Hello Kitty

The Remarkable Story of Sanrio and the Billion Dollar Feline Phenomenon

Hello Kitty

The Remarkable Story of Sanrio and the Billion Dollar Feline Phenomenon

KEN BELSON & BRIAN BREMNER

JOHN WILEY & SONS (ASIA) PTE LTD

Other Wiley Editorial Offices:
111 River Street, Hoboken, NJ, 07030, USA
The Atrium, Southern Gate, Chichester PO19 8SQ, England
John Wiley & Sons (Canada) Ltd, 22 Worcester Road, Rexdale, Ontario M9W 1L1,Canada
John Wiley & Sons Australia Ltd, 33 Park Road (PO Box 1226), Milton, Queensland 4064, Australia
Wiley – VCH, Pappelallee 3, 69469 Weinheim, Germany

Library of Congress Cataloging in Publication Data
ISBN 0-470-82094-2

Typeset in 12/14 point, Palatino by M.G. Dorett.
Printed in Singapore by Saik Wah Press Pte Ltd.
10 9 8 7 6 5 4 3 2

Contents

Acknowledgements

Growing up on Long Island in the 1970s, I discovered that my sister was hooked on a new set of toys: Hello Kitty. She had pencils, pads, purses, all girlish cute yet somehow appealing. Best of all, the stuff was affordable – a dollar here, $1.50 there. With money earned as a babysitter, I could buy some of the stuff to give her as gifts.

Flash forward to 1994, when my sister visited Japan. While wandering through a department store, I found her doubled over laughing in front of a Hello Kitty display. Like Arnold in the Terminator, Kitty was back.

Kitty remained our inside joke until 2001, when Wiley approached me to write this book. I was intrigued about the world's most famous cat, but had little time to organize such a project. Brian Bremner, my former boss at Business Week, convinced me otherwise. He didn't just encourage me, he took on half the project.

Dual authorship is no easy matter. Egos get in the way, writing styles differ and partners get sick of each other. None of that was the case with Brian. Not only is he a great writer, but he is a thoughtful friend and a serious thinker with a quick wit. His mellow demeanor balanced my frenzied pace. I can not imagine a better writing cohort.

We were fortunate to work with the folks at Wiley, especially Nick Wallwork who was the driver of the project, and Malar Manoharan, who was a reassuring and steady editor. Thanks to

Pauline Pek, who also helped us search for Nick. CJ Hwu did a great job banging the text into shape. Chris Newson and his team helped us with the marketing.

Kazuhide Yoneyama at the Sanrio headquarters deserves special mention. From the time we first met in August 2001, he handled my requests for information and interviews precisely, quickly and seriously. We received excellent cooperation from Tsuji-shacho on down. At no point did Sanrio try to vet our interviews or prevent us from writing anything.

Though I worked on this project in the evenings and on the weekends, thanks go to my colleagues at the New York Times. They were not involved directly with the book, but their help with my work at the newspaper made doing both projects possible.

Special thanks go to Chieko Tsuneoka, who did a first-rate job translating several crucial Japanese texts. Her diligence, knowledge of animation and experience working on books were both helpful and valuable.

There are too many friends to thank here for their encouragement and ideas (and promises to buy the book!). My family, too, stood by me even when we went long periods without meeting, time that I can not replace. My sister, in particular, was a constant inspiration and great help with contacts and ideas. My niece, Emma, with her closet full of Hello Kitty, proved our point that this cute cat has universal appeal.

My wife, Harumi, not only endured my endless hours in front of the computer, but put up with my obsession with Kitty. She was compassionate and supportive far beyond what I can possibly offer in return. This book is dedicated to her.

Ken Belson

My fascination with all things Hello Kitty comes from a different perspective than Ken. I had been vaguely aware of the Moon-faced one over the years, but had never really given the cat a passing thought. That all changed with the arrival of my two daughters— Marie and Elena—during the latter half of the 1990s. My education began with the arrival of Kitty-chan baby spoons, nappies, bibs, and t-shirts.

With each passing year, though, a deluge of Sanrio artifacts started showing up across our household. Then one Xmas Eve, on a last-minute shopping excursion with my wife, Yuki, I found myself shelling out $20 or so for a pink, Hello-Kitty-festooned vacuum cleaner for the little ones. It wasn't the shrewdest purchase of my life. But I knew the girls would be enraptured, for they were hooked on the brand and, in a weird way, I was, too.

Sorting all that out, plus the larger puzzle of why cuteness is something close to an aesthetic value in Japan, really got me thinking about Hello Kitty in a serious way. Deciding to work with Ken was a no-brainer. Simply put, he is one of the classiest acts that I have ever had the pleasure to work with. He is a top-flight journalist and a valued friend.

I second Ken's acknowledgment to the team at Wiley and the generous access that Sanrio granted us for this book. I'd like to thank Naoko Nishiwaki for her fine research work and also BusinessWeek Editor-in-Chief Steve Shepard for allowing me to take on this project. Finally, I'd like to dedicate this book to the cuties that bring much joy to my life: Yuki, Marie and Elena.

Brian Bremner

The Remarkable Story of

Hello Kitty...

Introduction

The Mouthless Cat that Roared

First time visitors to Japan are, in many ways, all alike, whether they come from the U.S., Germany or China. At first glance, they see Tokyo, the most frequent gateway for trips to Japan, as a buzzing yet orderly city crammed with offices, apartment blocks, restaurants and thousands of stores. The country's commercial might is on display: the streets are filled with trucks, taxis and cars, all seemingly filled with polite, purposeful drivers; legions of office workers dutifully file out of packed subway cars and into packed elevators that take them to their offices; the streets are spotless and the taxi drivers even wear white gloves. Everything seems to work.

Scratch a bit deeper, though, and you'll find a raucous media war going on. It's the fight for people's attention. Everywhere in this narrow country, citizens are bombarded with signs, symbols and all manner of come-ons. Some pitches are subtle and oblique, like pictures of famous pop stars plastered on billboards endorsing a product. Everyone knows they don't actually use it, but their face somehow lends the product some credibility. Words aren't needed, images seem to be enough. Sometimes, the pitch is unintentionally ironic, like the "Smokin' clean" logo of a smiling salaryman plastered on smoldering public ashtrays. Whatever the medium, it's clear Japanese are exposed to thousands of these messages everyday. In many ways, they have become oblivious to them, mostly out of necessity, like the grandmas walking past screaming bands of street hawkers handing out packets of tissues with advertisers' messages inside. But with so many companies putting so much energy into getting their pitch across, it's fair to say that Japanese have become some of the world's most sophisticated connoisseurs of signs and symbols. This makes sense in a country where non-verbal communication is often the preferred means of communication and the country's language is a series of pictograms called *kanji*. It also fits with Japan's long tradition of graphic arts – everything from scrolls, to water colors to woodblock prints, to *manga* (comic books) and *anime* (animated video) – Japanese love using images, artistic or otherwise, to communicate.

It makes sense then, that Japan has also produced one of the world's most successful commercial images, a demure cat called Hello Kitty. Mickey Mouse and Snoopy may be more famous and lucrative characters, thanks to a string of Disney movies and the long-running Peanuts comic strips. But Hello Kitty is pure imagery. With few exceptions, her creators at Sanrio Ltd. have purposely shied away from developing any story to her life, instead leaving her personality to the eyes and minds of the beholder. This Zen-like technique, intentionally or not, has allowed Kitty to become at once the princess of purity to toddlers, a cuddly playmate for young girls and a walk down memory lane for adults yearning for another taste of childhood. At the same time, Kitty has been vilified by anarcho-feminists, anti-consumer critics and others who see her as part of a devilish plot to sell worthless junk in a saccharine sweet package.

Whatever side of the argument you fall on, there's no denying that Kitty means business – big business. Although

Sanrio has a lineup of more than 400 different characters, Kitty, who was created in 1974, generates about half of Sanrio's $1 billion in annual sales. She is stuck on more than 20,000 products, about one-third produced by Sanrio and the rest licensed to outsiders (generating billions in more revenue) in every major economy on the globe. Her moon-shaped face has been slapped on every imaginable product: clothing and toys, of course, but also toasters, trashcans and, for a while, automobiles. She has spawned films, television shows and a newspaper, and has become one of the most coveted brand images in the world. Bill Gates thought so highly of Hello Kitty that he reportedly was willing to pay $5.6 billion to acquire her copyright.

Kitty is also part of Japan's growing – and increasingly global – entertainment industry, one that is worth between $400 billion and $500 billion a year, or up to 10% of the country's gross domestic product in 2002.[1] Whether it be *manga, anime,* video games or dozens of other media, Japan has been turned into a national Toon Town, a giant petri dish for the graphic arts. *Manga* alone generates $6 billion a year in sales, and 60% of the world's animated videos are produced in Japan. Companies like Sega, Nintendo and Sony have carved out a huge chunk of America's multi-billion dollar video game market. Sanrio, Bandai, Konami and others are doing the same in the toy market.

This book attempts to explain how all this came to be, and to posit where it is all headed. By looking at Hello Kitty, we hope to show that Sanrio stumbled onto one of the most ingenious formulas in the history of modern branding. By sticking her cute face on practically everything, Sanrio has created an entire commercial category where cute and consumers converge, often in unexpected ways. Though Japan is Kitty's home, her brand power has allowed her to spread throughout Asia and, more recently, to the U.S. and Europe. We'll find out why.

This transformation was not simply the result of slavish consumers getting sucked into a commercial maw. Kitty's success is part of the rise of what we call the "culture of cute," a unique blend of post-modern desire and infantile affectation. This, too, grew up first in Japan in the 1970s and 1980s and is now spreading overseas. Sanrio's founder, Shintaro Tsuji, was one of the first businessmen to tap into this market and one of the most skilled practitioners at mining his characters for millions.

Though Kitty remains hugely popular, she, like all brands, must be managed and massaged to remain profitable. And as she nears the end of her third decade in the public eye, there are signs that her appeal is starting to fade in some corners. Sanrio, like many companies, is scrambling to come up with alternative strategies for growing its business. In this way, Kitty represents an engaging and ongoing study in brand management. For decades, Sanrio has been steered by Tsuji's heavy hand. Born in 1927, Tsuji is nearing retirement and questions are emerging about whether the company has a strategy to replace his instincts and charisma. Indeed, how Sanrio deals with these challenges will help determine whether Kitty will remain one of the world's most recognizable images, or whether she will turn into cat litter and sequestered to the cartoon trash heap.

ENDNOTES

[1] Ronald Morse, Paul I. Terasaki Chair in U.S.-Japan Relations at UCLA, UCLA Asia Institute: The Battle for the Global Entertainment Industry: Japan's Growing Strength in Digital Culture, Jan. 2003 published article.

Chapter 1

Deconstructing Hello Kitty

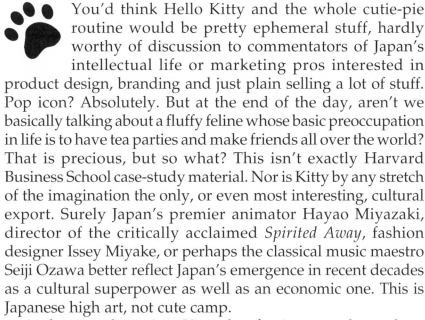 You'd think Hello Kitty and the whole cutie-pie routine would be pretty ephemeral stuff, hardly worthy of discussion to commentators of Japan's intellectual life or marketing pros interested in product design, branding and just plain selling a lot of stuff. Pop icon? Absolutely. But at the end of the day, aren't we basically talking about a fluffy feline whose basic preoccupation in life is to have tea parties and make friends all over the world? That is precious, but so what? This isn't exactly Harvard Business School case-study material. Nor is Kitty by any stretch of the imagination the only, or even most interesting, cultural export. Surely Japan's premier animator Hayao Miyazaki, director of the critically acclaimed *Spirited Away*, fashion designer Issey Miyake, or perhaps the classical music maestro Seiji Ozawa better reflect Japan's emergence in recent decades as a cultural superpower as well as an economic one. This is Japanese high art, not cute camp.

And yet, and yet, it is Kitty that fascinates and somehow hovers most visibly above the non-stop windstorm of ideas, fads, buzz and motifs that drives and shape Japanese popular

7

culture. Kitty beguiles on several levels. The most obvious one: How did a cartoon character so simple in design — a round head, button nose, a red ribbon and no mouth — achieve near cult-like status internationally as a fashion icon. Kitty lacks the pedigree, nostalgia factor and body of supporting television and film work going back to 1927 that gives one a pretty good idea of what Mickey Mouse is all about. Charles Schulz launched his Peanuts newspaper cartoon in 1950 and Snoopy emerged as a cleverly ironic character that one could track in a globally syndicated comic strip as well as television and film. Kitty by contrast was devised in 1974, and though there are assorted books and videos about her, the storyline has always been minimalist to the extreme. Also, for decades she wasn't much of a standout in the global character goods business.

The tipping point of her popularity in Japan didn't come until 1996 and in the mid 1990s her popularity surged in Asia and more recently in the U.S. and parts of Europe. Now by most metrics such as brand awareness and licensing fees, Kitty currently reigns as one of the undisputed leaders of Japan's $16 billion (2 trillion Yen) character goods business. There is something, dare we say it, so post-modern about Kitty. Surely, some enterprising cultural anthropologist at this very moment is deconstructing Kitty for an upcoming doctoral dissertation entitled, *Transforming The Boundaries: Symbolic Values and the Imagined Community of Hello Kitty.* At the risk of enraging French-influenced literary theorists the world over, we'll take a stab at a boilerplate definition of post-modernism as it applies to Kitty. Basically, the PoMo set believes that there are no ultimate truths about things. That's an illusion. Instead, how one views something — a piece of literature, history or vexing questions such as why Kitty and her twin sister Mimmy appear with mouths in videos, but sans mouths on store shelves — is heavily influenced by history, prevailing ideologies or otherwise socially constructed by bias, yearnings or whatever.

Kitty's designers at Sanrio in Tokyo gave her a birthplace in London. She weighs the same as three apples, likes to play in the forest, practice piano or bake. To ordinary Japanese, these are associations with what they imagine to be provincial English life. But to kids in Taiwan or Hong Kong, where Kitty is all the rage, the fur ball is decidedly Japanese. Political and fringe groups on the World Wide Web have hijacked Kitty's image for all sorts of reasons. One site entitled "Hello Kitty: Animal Rights for Beginners" tells its visitors that, "If you love Hello Kitty so much, you are ready to explore the deeper thoughts on all the other real fluffies." One is then encouraged to click on related links and view stomach-churning images of animal vivisection and the horrors of factory farming.[1] This isn't cute — trust us on this one.

Kitty's global success also debunks the entire notion that the globalization of culture automatically means "made in the U.S.A." To noted Japanophile, Douglas McGray, writing for the august *Foreign Policy* journal in mid-2002, Kitty is proof positive that Japan's cultural influence and relevance globally is on the rise. Japan's ability to project military force abroad may be hemmed in by a war-renouncing constitution, and its economic prowess greatly diminished since the 1980s, but Kitty and other cultural exports represent what foreign-policy wizards such as Joseph S. Nye Jr. of Harvard University call "soft power." McGray tips his hat to Kitty as an inspired bit of cultural fusion and suggests it's emblematic of the "genius behind Japanese cultural strength in a global era that has many countries nervous about cultural erosion."[2]

Others see her in a less flattering light. The cute chic Kitty embodies is encouraging Japanese women to play a submissive role. Feminists deplore the fact that Japanese teens, with their pink lipstick, butterfly hair bands and pastel colored threads, affect squeaky voices, pout their lips and stamp their feet when they are angry and purposely act clueless. All this is really about the male cultural domination and exploitation of women in Japan. It encourages girls and young women well into their late 20s to act submissive, weak and innocent rather than mature, assertive and independent. And there is no denying that ultra-cutie girls, especially those sporting Prussian-style school uniforms oddly enough, are a steady staple in Japanese pornography.

The fascinating thing about Kitty is that for a cat with no mouth, she manages both to speak to a global audience and say different things to different people. And from a strategic marketing point of view — at least in this case — saying less is definitely more when it comes to developing this brand.

JAPAN AS TOON TOWN

Viewed from a different perspective, Hello Kitty also says a lot about the country from which she emerged — Japan. But to understand just how deep the connections run, you really need to delve into Japan's unique cute culture or what they call *kawaii bunka*. The Japanese worship cuteness in all of its forms. What Kitty is really emblematic of isn't just a passing fashion statement, but something closer to an aesthetic value that runs extremely deep in the society and gender roles, particularly among women. So take an insulin shot and read on.

Any visitor to Japan circa 2003, at least not one on heavy medication, couldn't help but notice that "cute" is an omni-present force in Japan. The everyday landscape of Tokyo — the ad banners on the subways, storefront signs, digital display screens and various forms of mass media like *manga* and fashion magazines — are just oozing with the stuff. Sometimes it is the form of cartoon characters that are often used as pitchmen for all manner of Japanese products. A broad array of consumer-product companies, financial service outfits, even the government, has licensed cartoon characters to jazz up their advertising. On the packed Keio train line that takes thousands of commuters back and forth everyday from downtown to Tokyo's sprawling western suburbs, Hello Kitty warns straphangers not to lean against the door. All Nippon Airways decorates the exterior of some of its Boeing 747s with characters from Pokemon. Police stations in the Ginza look like gingerbread houses.

There are love hotels in Tokyo, designed like little fairy kingdoms, which charge by the hour and are a meeting point of choice for sexual liaisons. Middle-aged women working at ritzy, upscale department stores such as Takashimaya and Mitsukoshi don Pikachu and Miffy pins. And it isn't unusual to see Japan's corporate warrior engrossed in an adult *manga* featuring an ultra-cutie heroine character in some mildly pornographic storyline. The coterie of cuddliness even extends to Japan's Defense Agency, which has baby-faced soldiers as mascots in its promotional literature. One half expects that Kitty will some day show up on the side of one of Japan's Aegis-class destroyers.

The typical anatomy of cute characters such as Kitty, in the words of one authority on the subject, is "small, soft, infantile, mammalian, round, without bodily appendages (arms), without bodily orifices (mouths), non-sexual, mute, insecure, helpless or bewildered."[3] Spend five minutes in high-intensity retail centers like Shibuya and Shinjuku, and you almost feel like you are in toon town. Cute sells big time in Nippon. And there is just no escaping this slightly surreal world of Japanese character land. For Japan is kind of a marketer's paradise, the population density and space compression of the country's major urban centers such as Tokyo, Osaka, Nagoya and Yokohama mean Japanese get bombarded with cute messages just about everywhere they turn. One observer put it particularly well:

> Japanese have more information thrown at them than any other group of people in history. The word "blitz" does not adequately describe the situation. Along with national, regional and local newspapers, there are several hundred weekly and monthly magazines; a quarter

million public buses and train cars with hundreds of posters; half million taxicabs with places for advertising brochures; billboard trucks that exist only for advertising; public address systems in most large department stores; and more lights, signs, flashing announcements, and electrical displays through the Ginza, Roppongi, Shinjuku, Shibuya, Akasaka, Ikebukuro, or Asakusa, all with the underlying message, buy, buy, buy.[4]

JAPAN'S CULT OF CUTE

Naturally enough, cute fashion and values are heavily reinforced by mass market fashion and glamour magazines that carry messages (shaped by their major advertisers) of how Japanese women ought to look and manipulate their bodies through diet, exercise, plastic surgery and so on. If you want to quickly grasp what cute chic is all about in Japan, just pick up any one of the 30-plus magazines devoted to teen fashion or perhaps a *manga*, which features female heroines. One of the bibles of Japan's cute chic is *Cawaii!* magazine. The name is a play on the Japanese word for cute, *kawaii*. It has a circulation of about 300,000 and it targets 15- to 19-year-olds. There is a sister publication called *S Cawaii!* (as in *Senior Cawaii!*) to reach the older readers in their early 20s. After reading through several issues, it is not hard to catch on to the formula. On the cover is a pop diva like Ayumi Hamasaki or fashion models of the moment like Mayumi Sada. They look the part of girl seductress, gazing directly into the camera with lips slightly parted. They are thin and usually clad in a heavy dose of pastel colors and accessorized to the max with some sort of cute motif, be it butterflies or teddy bears.

Somewhat surprisingly, the editor-in-chief at *Cawaii!* isn't a woman, but a balding middle-aged guy named Kazuhiko Sato. He's in his late 40s, and was a sociology major at Waseda University during the mid-1970s. Back in those days, the cute look didn't exist and Sato dreamed of being a serious writer of note. In 1968 and 1969, Japan's entire university system was paralyzed by a radical student movement, which no doubt drew inspiration from the U.S. and Europe. The movement swept through 152 universities and resulted in 10,000 arrests. Students at Waseda and elsewhere raged against American involvement in Vietnam, a hike in tuition fees and alleged corruption by university leaders. But the movement took an ugly turn. Student protesters started to get identified with the terrorist Japanese Red Army, which launched a series of bombings and hijackings in the early 1970s. When it became clear Corporate Japan would blackball students with a prison record or radical political views, Sato's generation lost interest in politics. "Everyone became interested in tennis," he said.[5]

These days Sato finds himself ordering up pieces for his readers on skin care, tips for breast enhancement and the fashion trend of the moment, which in the summer of 2002 seemed to be the exposed mid-riff look. How the cute look has endured and adapted to churn-and-burn fashion cycles among Japanese teens intrigues Sato. Over the last 10 years, several fashion manias have come and gone. A rough, and by no means inclusive, list would include the urban rap or hip-hop look, the nonchalant American denim look, the bleached blonde and overly tanned look, the retro 1970s look with bell-bottoms and on and on. But there is always some cute element, modification or accessory that makes it distinctively Japanese. "It always floats above several fashion trends," mused Sato.

One interesting feature of *Cawaii!* editorial operations is that most of the models are recruited directly from the streets of fashion enclaves like Shibuya, Harajuku or Yoyogi Park, where tens of thousands of Japanese teens circulate every day. *Cawaii!* spotters invite girls with just the right look to pose in the magazine. Others compete in contests in which their photos are selected in a massive model audition. Any given issue of *Cawaii!* has 200 or so amateur models and they are clustered around certain fashion themes such as Hippie Girl, Lovely Girl or Summer Resort Gal. What's striking though is regardless of whether they are wearing bikinis or a traditional summer robe called a *yukata,* the girls tend to be wearing glossy lipstick and striking cute poses in front of the camera, such as pouting dramatically, placing a finger on one's chin, wrinkling up their noses and so on. Sato, for one, thinks cute power will be around Japan a very long time, and he doesn't think there is anything unhealthy or subversive about any of this. He rejects the concerns of feminists and has a unifying theory of his own about why cute is so powerful among Japanese girls. His take: "I don't think they are acting in a submissive way at all. They are trying to be cute to get more attention from the boys."

Keiko Horiki, the editor-in-chief at *AnAn* magazine, suggested that Japanese women prefer a flowery and cute look to the overtly sexy look of their counterparts in Europe and the U.S. "Japanese women are shy," she pointed out, "we don't go out with Japanese men to buy underwear together like they do in the West."[6] Horiki added that cute fashion, or at least a kind of androgynous look, has also taken grip of Japanese boys and young men. In the summer of 2002, the fad among Japanese guys involved shaving one's legs for the short-pants season. *AnAn* boasts a circulation of 400,000 and its target readership is women between the ages of 18 to 30 or so.

Of course, money is the rocket fuel of cute culture in Japan. It targets a trend-happy and relatively affluent sector of the female consumer market. As of Japan's 2000 population census, there were 64 million women and within that universe of consumers, there were 16.9 million, or some 26% of the total, between the ages of 15 and 34. In the 25 to 34 age cohort, 54% of the women nationally and 65% in the Tokyo metropolitan area are single. The trend toward Japanese women marrying later in life has been underway for the last decade or so. Cute fashion has a broad consumer market to live off of in Japan.

WHERE DID THE MADNESS COME FROM?

And yet, the cute craze wasn't necessarily dreamed up by some clever marketers at Sanrio and other consumer-goods companies and then imposed by some all-powerful and manipulative mass media on unsuspecting Japanese girls. In a way, it would be nice to think so. Hello Kitty critics, perhaps those with a leaning for mind-control conspiracies cooked up by advertising creative types and magazine editors, would have someone to blame. Then, the mystery of Kitty's popularity wouldn't be much of a mystery at all. Instead, it looks like Japan's whole *kawaii* cultural movement began kind of in a burst of spontaneity in the early 1970s, spawned from handwriting and linguistic fads.

Perhaps the best and most original analysis of the history of all things *kawaii* in Japan came in 1995 courtesy of Sharon Kinsella, a Cambridge University researcher who published a piece entitled *Cuties in Japan* in a much overlooked book of essays called *Women, Media and Consumption in Japan*. It starts out with a pretty fascinating point about the word *kawaii*. *Kawaii* is one of those rare all-purpose words that is repeated almost robotically day in and day out. The positive meanings of the word — cute, adorable, lovable and small — are what Hello Kitty is all about. Even foreign Japanese speakers start to say it reflexively after living in Japan for a while. It is probably the most widely used, or overused word, in modern Japanese. (By the way, its variant *kawaiiso* means pathetic, poor or great discomfort.) But when Kinsella consulted Japanese dictionaries from the first half of the 20th century, she noticed the word didn't exist in its current form. Back in those days, the best word for cute and adorable was *kawayushi* which later morphed into *kawayui*. *Kawaii* didn't really come of age until the early 1970s, when Japan's evolution as a rich and consumer-driven economy was impossible to deny.

Back then, something weird started to happen to Japanese girls, at least from the conservative viewpoint of Japanese cultural guardians. Time was, Japanese kids spent most of the primary school years learning the three sets of symbols that comprise the Japanese language, *hiragana*, *katakana* and at least 800 to 1,000 of the basic Chinese characters called *kanji*. (By the time they graduate from high school, students are expected to have mastered closer to 2,000 *kanji* characters.) Japanese kids spend countless hours writing and rewriting these linguistic building blocks to exact specification. There are established rules for the sequence of strokes, their arc and so on. Even to this day, sloppy penmanship will draw sharp rebukes from elderly Japanese of a conservative bent. It is considered somewhat boorish and even disrespectful to depart from the script.

So imagine the reaction when an entire generation of Japanese girls about 30 years ago started to defile the language with cute and purposely distorted Japanese characters. Explained Kinsella:

> Previously Japanese writing had been written vertically using strokes that vary in thickness along their length. The new style was written laterally, preferably using a mechanical pencil to produce very fine even lines. Using extremely stylized, rounded characters with English, *katakana* and little cartoon pictures such as hearts, stars and faces inserted randomly into the text, the new style of handwriting was distinct and its characters difficult to read. In middle and high schools across the country, the craze for writing in the new style caused discipline problems. In some schools the writing was banned entirely, or tests, which were completed using the new cute style, would not be marked.[7]

If this so-called *burikko* (fake-child writing) movement wasn't subversive enough to the old guard, the baby-talk craze that kicked off around the same time really set them off. Kids started deliberately mispronouncing Japanese words to make the sound cuter. As Kinsella noted, nobody better represented that debasing of the Japanese language than 1980s pop idol Sakai Noriko, who kicked off a fad called *Norippigo* in which the last syllable of common everyday adjectives was subbed for the "pi" sound. For instance, the word for happy, *ureshii*, became *ureppi*. It sounded cuter that way. Even new sexual slang emerged: The childish phrase *nyan nyan suru* (to meow, meow like a little kitty cat) took on the meaning of having sexual intercourse. *Norippigo* has died out, but not the practice of manipulating language to make it sound more adorable. These days at primary schools around Tokyo, it's not uncommon for schoolyard crushes to be described as *lub-lub-yu* a bit of Japlish to say "I love you" in an innocent, child-like way.

And though Japanese popular music, or J-pop as it is often short-handed, is quite a broad waterfront of styles — from the mildly punk look of the male hard-rock group Glay to the soulful diva Misia — record companies continue to rely on ultra-cute formula girl groups and female solo acts. They often feature dolled-up singers barely past pubescence in some mildly sexually suggestive outfit belting out overly sentimental, bubble-gum love songs with each cutie dancing out some choreographed routine. Even in 2003, girl groups like Morning Musume were striking the same sort of cute poses that would not seem unfamiliar to someone now in their 40s who grew up listening to a duo like Pink Lady in the 1970s or Seiko Matsuda, another piece of J-Pop candy from the 1980s. (Matsuda, however, became less of a cute idol among the gossip magazines in the 1990s for her extramarital activities and two divorces.)

A YEN FOR CUTENESS

Perhaps there is something in the drinking water in Japan that fosters a fascination, if not obsession, with all things cute among girls of a certain age. This certainly isn't unique to

Japan, but it is hard to think of any parallels in the rich world that matches this kind of intensity. And while this trend sprung from somewhere deep in the psyche of Japan's 1970s youth culture, it wasn't long before commerce and market researchers caught on and started commercially exploiting this trend. And no company has done that better than Sanrio under the direction of its founder and President Shintaro Tsuji.

From 1960s, Sanrio started infusing cute designs on kid's stationery and then moved on into dreamy schoolgirl diaries, pens and what later became known as fancy goods in Japan. They were inexpensive, ultra-precious knick-knacks that young girls could buy for themselves or perhaps give away as gifts. But to really juice up the sugar levels, you really needed cartoon characters, he figured. And Tsuji over the ensuing decade (and still into the present) ordered his team of designers to crank them out prodigiously in the hope of spawning a commercial phenomenon. So year after year, out of Sanrio's central casting department, came a whole legion of adorable, cutesy-wootsy, itty-bitty creatures such as Strawberry King, Cheery Chums, Button Nose and, of course, Hello Kitty. Though Tsuji, like any good businessman, is in the business of making tons of money, he would cast his strategy as one of promoting "social communication" in Japan.

By that he primarily meant creating an array of relatively inexpensive fancy goods — priced at no more than $10 and small tokens of friendship that are fun to have around — that will play to the natural human instinct to make some sort of personal connection with others or perhaps fulfill a social obligation. By the start of the 1990s, Sanrio and a host of other companies such as toymaker Bandai and other consumer-goods makers that licensed comic characters from Japan and abroad had made a profound impact on Japanese marketing. Walk into the home or condo of any typical Japanese nuclear family with one or two kids, and you'd likely see a household brimming with cute items — stickers, pens, stationery, toiletry items, toothbrushes and cups, saucers, chopsticks and scads of toys and kids clothing — promoting one character or another. Cuteness represented a breakthrough product design development for Corporate Japan. It was kind of Japan's answer to the fact that with the arrival of an industrialized, mass consumption economy life gets faster, less connected to nature, more depersonalized and somewhat alienating. Surrounding yourself with cute things could offset that a little, bringing some whimsy and comfort into one's life, lending a subjective quality to otherwise sterilized products like a vacuum cleaner, microwave oven or rice cooker. Modern consumers, adult men and women, and not just the kids, started to incorporate some of this whimsy and humor into their everyday purchasing habits.

In asking why this eruption took place in Japan, two things stand out. At the take-off stage of any cute character, Japanese youths are key. And in Japan, starting in the early 1970s, kids growing up in fairly affluent families in major urban centers such as Tokyo, Osaka and Nagoya were lavished, emotionally and financially. On the first point, a survey of one private high school in Tokyo, conducted by the Hakuhodo Institute of Life and Living in the late 1990s, found that students received allowances ranging from $50 to $200 a month. On top of that, parents, grandparents and other close relatives often present cash gifts, known as *otoshidama*, during the New Year holidays. Naturally enough, Japanese kids, like their counterparts in the U.S. and Europe, tend to spend that loot on items promoted as cute, cool or otherwise desirable by the mass media.

Secondly, Japan has a very deeply entrenched gift-giving culture that serves as a motivating force to buy and exchange fancy goods. And for a long-running character such as Kitty, there is also a nostalgia factor that drives its sales among mothers and other women. As for gift-giving occasions, they are aplenty. Japan is in many ways a giant favor bank. Every small act of generosity must later be paid back in kind. And woe to the ingrate who takes more than he or she gives back.

Imported Western holidays like Christmas and Valentine's Day are actually secondary gift-giving occasions but still important. There are year-end (*seibo*) and mid-year (*chugen*) corporate present-swapping seasons. And in polite society, there are gifts for the sick or victims of misfortune (*mimai*); souvenirs brought back from trips (*miyage*); and presents for happy developments like a big promotion (*shugi*). There are even funeral gifts called *koden*, typically cash tucked into a decorative envelop. The bereaved family is required to return a gift equivalent to one-third to one-half the value of the *koden*, according to Japanese etiquette manuals. True, you probably wouldn't want to present matching Hello Kitty hand towels at a funeral, but the cheer-me-up quality of many cute goods does seem to work well in a number of Japanese social occasions as well as required paybacks for small favors rendered such as watching a neighbor's daughter for a few hours or celebrating the birth of a baby and so on.

HELLO KITTY AND GIRL POWER?

By now, some might be wondering if there isn't something a little over the top about all this. Hello Kitty is precious and all that, but why would that matter to, say, anyone past the age of 10? In the U.S., little girls value cute things. They are also more interested in developing communication and socialization skills just like Japanese girls and identifying themselves by a brand like Hello Kitty, a particular look, pop idol and so on. But, generally speaking, by the age of 10 or so, they start to experiment with different looks and leave Hello Kitty in the toy chest. In Japan, by contrast, aspiring to some sort of cute look extends well into the middle-school and high-school years. Even young women well into their 20s sometimes take their voice up a half octave, affect innocent expressions and childish embarrassment when interacting with men or in the workplace.

Not surprisingly, not everyone sees Hello Kitty and the values this cat represents as in the best interest of Japanese society. Cultural critics since the late 1980s have linked the cute aesthetic with crass consumerism, the debasement of the work ethic, the infantalization of Japanese youth, and a general rebellion against the whole post-war Japanese societal compact that values conformism, discipline, self-sacrifice and deference to authority. Back in 1986, noted University of Tokyo-trained sociologist Osamu Nakano published a scathing critique of Japanese youth culture in a piece entitled "A Sociological Analysis of the New Breed" in the conservative journal *Seiron*. In it, he raged against a generation inebriated with childishness and consumerism:

> In considering the personality traits of the new breed, the first characteristic we note is they are 'moratorium people' — that is, they do not want to grow up. It is not that they cannot but that they do not even try. They repudiate the maturity demanded by the norms of adult society and prefer to remain kids — a dramatic contrast with the members of the previous generation, who became anxious to attain full-fledged adulthood, when they reached the age of 20 or so. To be sure, the ability to remain kids presupposes the overprotection made possible by affluence, but it seems to me that the moratorium psychology also signifies repugnance toward the values underlying and created by modern society.[8]

Though Nakano wasn't talking specifically about Japanese women, he might as well have been. Because, as he wrote, a trend was well underway in which Japanese women continued to delay getting married, living at home or in nearby apartments, spending money not just on fancy goods but also foreign travel and pretty much living the high life. Young women came to dominate and drive forward pop culture trends, not surprising given that they kept spending while the economy generally stagnated during the 1990s. Single Japanese women also came to be somewhat resented for enjoying the freest and most unencumbered lifestyles on the archipelago. They represented a threat to the whole post-war definition of female gender roles in Japan. The idealized vision of young, urban 20-something Japanese women went something like this: Work as an "office lady" doing low-level clerical work, merely a temporary arrangement until one could find a suitable mate. In the meantime, young ladies would master the so-called "bridal arts" such as highly ritualized tea ceremonies, flower arrangement, cooking and maintaining and wearing kimonos. Summed up one observer:

> For young middle-class women, bridal arts have also provided tuition in the 'good wife, wise mother' ideal which contributes to their value on the marriage market, at the same time preparing them for a married life of idle boredom and the bliss of Japanese-ness.[9]

Yet somewhere along the way, young Japanese women started to renege on the deal. Hello Kitty and the cute movement, devoted as they are to escapism, consumerism, whimsy and nostalgia, clearly represented a threat to reigning ideology that women best served their society and families by attending to their kids' education and running households in such a way their spouses could devote themselves to work and late-night drinking sessions in Ginza. Increasingly, young Japanese women preferred to covet their independence for as long as biologically possible — say, well into their 30s — before having to make a life-altering choice about whether to pursue motherhood or not. By 2000, Japanese conservatives coined a new phrase for Japanese women in their late 20s and early 30s who had gone completely AWOL on the whole idea of being married with kids — at least until they were good and ready. A bestseller by Tokyo Gakugei University professor Masahiro Yamada was entitled *Parasaito Shinguru No Jidai*, or the *Age of the Parasite Single*.

Sounds like a B-grade horror flick, doesn't it? And to Japanese demographers, it might as well be. The phrase refers to "spoiled singles" living at home well into young adulthood, paying little in the way of rent, and jetting off to Maui for a week of indolence on the beach instead of doing something productive like changing nappies. Aside from the moralists who think these kids are world-class slackers, the government sees the trend as a big reason behind Japan's declining birth rate. For instance, the percentage of women who are unmarried in the 25- to 29-year-old age group, many of whom live with their parents, has doubled over the past 15 years, to 48% in 1998. Unless more young Japanese choose marriage and childrearing, the theory goes, Japan will face some tough choices. With the country's workforce rapidly aging, editorialists are already calling for a radical new approach to immigration. That would indeed be a shocker for Japan.

Still, this blow to *kawaii* culture and the tendency of Japanese women to value the freedom and comforts of staying single for as long as possible primarily comes from a circle of older and somewhat embittered intellectuals cloistered away at universities, and conservative journals who are appalled by the direction Japan is heading. They also don't get the joke. Without quite knowing it, Japan has experienced the subtle emergence of a girl-power movement over the last several decades and Hello Kitty, at the symbolic level, is leading the way. Sure, Japanese men control the political and economic structures and all the trappings of power that come with that, but it is the young unattached, urban working woman who enjoys the most personal freedom in this highly structured society. She floats from job to job, travels often and typically has the kind of disposable income to buy a Gucci handbag. Hello Kitty and cute or frivolous consumption are about feeling good and carefree. In that sense, Hello Kitty is a menace, a Bolshevik with a bomb, a threat to the established value system.

And yet Japanese girls just want to have fun. To some, this is really all about the love of cuteness in and of itself.

In February 2002, *The New York Times Magazine* fashion editor Amy M. Spindler, made a surprising claim that Tokyo, not New York, Milan or Paris, is the true international fashion capital. Not by the usual metrics of dollar volume, the density of designers, suppliers, models, media focus and so on, but by the sheer devotion of the society to the ephemeral, floating world of fashion. Japanese consumers have a special talent for rapidly importing one international fashion trend after another, stripping it of any political or rebellious meaning, infusing it with *kawaii* values and creating an entirely different fashion statement of their own. Marveled Spindler:

> Unlike the London punks or the mods, or the New York rappers who so inspire dress in the streets of Japan's capital, there are no politics behind the Tokyo fashion movements. The punk movement, when it came, was only about fashion. The hip-hop movement has nothing to do with rebellion. Boystyle has nothing to do with women's rights. If you ask girls why they are wearing it, it's because 'it's cute.' What are those sartorial movements without anger? Well, they're happy clothes, they're *kawaii*.[10]

AMBASSADOR KITTY

For an executive like Sanrio patriarch Tsuji, *kawaii* values that Hello Kitty embodies — innocence, sentimentality and harmony — also tie in somewhat with the current ideology in Japan about its role in the world or at least the imagined or idealized image it would like to portray in the world. Perhaps because of his trying childhood and psychological make-up, Tsuji is basically an idealist at heart. Just as Kitty desires deeply to be loved, trusted and respected, so does Japan, he argued. "In the bubble era, when Japan made money on an unprecedented scale, it didn't receive much respect from people of the world," he said.[11] In fact, during the 1970s and 1980s as Japan took leadership positions in one core manufacturing industry after another while keeping its economy relatively closed to imports, the West viewed the country as a threat. Japan seemed to have perfected a new form of capitalism based on Japanese values of consensus, state-directed lending, quality circles and government intervention that the U.S. couldn't match. Back then, it wasn't Hello Kitty that symbolized Japan, but Godzilla. Worse, all the success bred a certain national swagger that created anxiety and mistrust abroad. One only has to recall the near-racist portrayal of Japanese business and society in Michael Crichton's caricature-driven murder thriller *Rising Sun*.

Of course, Japan's bubble economy and the whole riff about the superiority of the Japanese way ended in tears. For Japan, the 1990s added up to a dreary decade of recessions, political corruption and paralysis, anxiety about the economic ascendance of China and hectoring from the U.S. and other allies about its sick banking sector and ineffectual policies. But it was also a period when Japanese culture — once routinely ridiculed for its unrivaled insularity — started to have a coming-out party of sorts. Film directors such as Takeshi (Beat) Kitano developed a following in Europe, while J-Pop stars such as Namie Amuro and others climbed the music charts in Hong Kong, Taiwan and Singapore. Hello Kitty, Pokemon, karaoke and Nintendo video games drawing from Japan's *manga* genre made big inroads into the U.S. Turns out Japan does have something else to offer the world other than managerial doctrines about quality and just-in-time delivery. It has developed a vibrant pop culture that can more than hold its own in the global marketplace for ideas, buzz and fashion. Hello Kitty is perhaps the most obvious example, but scarcely the only one. Summed up McGray quoted elsewhere in this chapter:

> Gradually, over the course of an otherwise dismal decade,
> Japan has been perfecting the art of transmitting certain

kinds of mass culture — a technique that has contributed mightily to U.S. hegemony around the world. If Japan sorts out its economic mess and military angst, and if younger Japanese become secure in asserting their own values and traditions, Tokyo can regain the role it briefly assumed at the turn of the 19th century, when it simultaneously sought to engage the West and to become a military and cultural power on its own terms.

Whether Japan will reach the sunny uplands of confident national identity and long-term economic prosperity that McGray pictures, could well be the subject of another book, but there is something to the case that Japanese culture has grown more, not less, competitive. And Hello Kitty seems very much in sync with the current national mood. Japan isn't considered a hegemony on the world stage, it has a war-renouncing constitution and likes to see itself as a force for peace and harmony around the globe. Indeed, months after the September 11 terrorist attacks in the U.S., Hello Kitty was portrayed as a peacemaker in a very sentimental musical staged at Sanrio Puroland, a company-owned theme park in suburban Tokyo. In the story line, which Tsuji personally signed off on, costumed and stereotypical figures representing the U.S., the Middle East, Europe and China come to blows and then resolve their conflict after Hello Kitty stamps her feet and sings a song about friendship.

Add it all up. The mind-boggling thing about Hello Kitty is how such a minimalist format and message can have so many meanings, delighting some and perhaps revolting others. Whether Hello Kitty will be showing up on all manner of knick-knacks, consumer goods and marital aids 50 years from now is an open question. But the Hello-Kitty wave does offer up some fascinating questions about why some global brands thrive and others don't. To really understand the roots of her global success so far one must go beyond traditional marketing concepts about brand management and start thinking about how culture is transmitted across boundaries, not just physical but also mental. There is something about Hello Kitty that has traction. Say what you want about her, but this is one deep cat.

ENDNOTES

[1] The website for Hello Kitty Animal Right for Beginners can be found at http://geocities.com/ripana/hellokitty.html.

[2] Douglas McGray, "Japan's Gross National Cool," Foreign Policy, May/June 2002.

[3] Sharon Kinsella, "Cuties in Japan," Women Media and Consumption in Japan, ed. Lise Skov & Brian Moeran (Honolulu: University of Hawaii Press, 1995) 224

[4] Colin Ducolon, "Small and Cute Sells: The Marketing of Toys and Games in Japan," 1999. This Keizai Koho Fellowship essay can be found at http://kkcfellowships.ncss.org/1999articles.

[5] Kazuhiko Sato, Editor-in-Chief, *Cawaii!* magazine, personal interview, June 12, 2002.

[6] Keiko Horiki, Editor-in-Chief, AnAn, personal interview, June 12, 2002.

[7] See Kinsella's "Cuties in Japan," 222.

[8] Osamu Nakano, "Shinjinrui Genron," published in Seiron, Nov. 1986. The article was translated and later published in 1988 by Japan Echo, Volume XV.

[9] Lise Skov & Brian Moeran, "Hiding in the Light," 25, in Women Media and Consumption in Japan (Honolulu: University of Hawaii Press, 1995).

[10] Amy M. Spindler, "Do You Otaku?," The New York Times Magazine, Feb. 24, 2002.

[11] Translated from Shintaro Tsuji, "Kore ga Sanrio no Himitsu Desu" (The Secrets of Sanrio), March 2002 by Fusosha, Tokyo, 36.

Chapter 2

The God of Kawaii

Like pop idols and sports stars honed in the art of the media interview, Shintaro Tsuji has learned to answer the most obvious questions in an engaging way. Rather than huff and snort at softball questions, Tsuji, the founder and president of Sanrio Ltd., makes the interviewer feel that in some small way he is thinking of the reply for the first time. Shy as a kid, he has become a smooth and sharp salesman. Tsuji makes his responses – which he has formulated after years of practice – sound spontaneous and plausible. Why, he is asked, is Hello Kitty so popular?

The question is a bit like asking why do kids go gaga over Mickey Mouse or Snoopy? Who can explain such things? So, with a certain amount of modesty and a dash of wonder, Tsuji says he doesn't have the slightest idea why Hello Kitty, a white cartoon cat with an outsized head, shrunken body and expressionless face could be worth half a billion dollars. Sensing that Tsuji, a man who has spent nearly three decades promoting the cat, is feigning innocence, the interviewer tries to elicit a more revealing answer. Tsuji lies in wait for the obvious follow-up question. Well, he says, warming up to the moment, people of all ages love the chronically cute cat because her soft features and inviting colors put them at ease. The cat, you see, has the right blend of whites, pinks and reds. Her poses are simple yet seductive. Her blank look and lack of a mouth engender comfort and let people project on to her whatever they want.

The interviewer nods in agreement, but is still left puzzled. Sanrio has 450 other animated characters in its stable all with roughly the same characteristics, yet none are nearly as successful as Hello Kitty, which is sold in 40 countries and plastered on more than 20,000 different products, everything from pens to toasters.

So Tsuji makes a show of fumbling for more scientific answers. He rolls out his concept of "social communication," whereby friends give friends cuddly gifts that smooth over the rough edges in life and help cement relationships. In this context, Kitty's innocuous charm becomes a magnet drawing people to give her as a gift. What's more, Kitty has been around so long – nearly three decades and counting – that girls who grew up with her have become reacquainted with her in adulthood as they seek ways to "return to their youth." These same women are now mothers who are buying Kitty monogrammed blankets and wallpaper for their children's bedrooms.

"Kitty-chan has been loved for such a long time because friendship is something eternal," Tsuji said.[1]

Eventually, though, Tsuji winds his way back to the beginning: How did this simple character become one of the most unique and popular icons in the world? Part businessman, part devout believer, Tsuji shrugs his shoulders in amazement. His instinct tells him not to probe much deeper into why he has had the good fortune to turn a cartoon design into a world-class brand. At 75, Tsuji remains honest enough to marvel at the hand he's been dealt.

"In 35 years, Sanrio has made 450 characters," Tsuji said.[2] "But, of course, really only one was a real hit: Kitty.

The longest of the characters lasted for just seven years, but only Kitty has lasted longer. I have no idea why Kitty has lasted this long," Tsuji says.

Though his collection of answers is not the cosmic satori you hoped would calm your karma, Tsuji certainly has plenty of qualities worth marveling at. He and his company, a 43 year-old outfit with headquarters in Tokyo, have worked years not only to develop Hello Kitty, but also to preserve and defend her. As stewards of a drawing easily replicated, they not only market her relentlessly, but also vigorously protect her from copyright infringements, rip-off artists and renegades on the Internet.

At the same time, in trying to make money off her – and there's tons to be made – they walk a fine line between maintaining her popularity and turning her into a fad that will fade away in months. They also balance the need to splash her on everything from stationery to washers, yet not water down her image by putting her on cheap-quality items. "It's like a balloon," Tsuji said . "If you keep blowing it up, eventually it will pop."[3]

In this delicate dance, Tsuji and his company have been masterful. Sanrio is the largest character-goods company in Japan's $16.7 billion[4] market – no mean feat in a country crowded with messages and in love with animation. Tsuji pioneered the use of copyrights and trademarks in characters nearly four decades ago, importing American characters and toys like Barbie, Betty Boop and the Pink Panther[5], as well as designing his own. Sanrio has also brought Kitty and her cast of friends to a country near you, making an impact throughout Asia, North America and increasingly in Europe and South America. In doing so, the cat has become a Japanese goodwill ambassador, one of Japan's most recognizable cultural exports. The cat's brand is so treasured that Microsoft Corp. Chairman Bill Gates, through an intermediary, offered Tsuji $5.6 billion for the rights to Hello Kitty.[6] Microsoft denies the claim and anyway, Tsuji laughed it off and turned him down.[7]

No, the Hello Kitty phenomenon, despite its quiet birth in 1974, its initial rise, disappearance and then rebirth in the 1990s, is no fluke. With foresight and cleverness, Tsuji has taken the original concept of the cat to heights few could have predicted. He also, like many successful entrepreneurs, was not afraid to experiment and was not halted by failures, but in fact driven to bounce back.

To get this far, though, Tsuji, like any entrepreneur, had to have the drive and desire to work at a relentless pace. To maintain his bottomless enthusiasm for promoting Hello Kitty, Tsuji not only had to love the product, but also find meaning in it. And indeed Tsuji has and does. Hello Kitty and many of its altered states are a product of Tsuji's life. In fact, few company founders are as closely intertwined with their products as Tsuji and Kitty. Through his more than four decades heading Sanrio, Tsuji has attempted to exorcise the demons of his cheerless childhood by trying to spread happiness, efforts that are manifested in the cat and the love it is meant to represent. His good nature and very outgoing (and un-Japanese) friendliness match Kitty's perpetual cheerfulness.

The two are so bound together that they even look out for each other, metaphorically speaking. Tsuji's human foibles – his artistic impulse, his entrepreneurial risk taking, his sometimes obsessive trust in the stock market – have strained the company's finances often. Yet more than any co-worker, Kitty, like the friend she's supposed to be, has bailed Tsuji out.

This is not to dismiss the power of Tsuji's intuition or his business acumen. But it does suggest that to understand the power of the mouthless cat, you have to understand Tsuji and the twists and turns of his life that led to Kitty's birth and their mutual rise to global stardom. In other words, you have to go back to the beginning and pull together the strands of Tsuji's life that have been woven into Hello Kitty.

YAMANASHI – LIVING ON WITS AND BRAWN

More than most modern nations, Japan is a country where its people closely identify with the place they are born. Mountains cover about three-quarters of these narrow islands. In olden days, before bullet trains and jet travel, many regions were geographically and culturally distinct. Japan's medieval government was really a collection of fiefdoms that for centuries fought vicious civil wars to defend their mountain valleys, seaside coves and coveted plains. Even in modern times, Japanese still puff up when talking of their hometown, spicing up their speech with the local dialect and talk of their favorite local dish.

Television, a centralized education system and the migration away from rural districts and toward urban centers have eroded some pride of place. But Shintaro Tsuji grew up before many of these transitional forces reshaped the country, so in many ways, he still bears the qualities that mark his birthplace.

Born in Kofu, Yamanashi prefecture on December 7, 1927, Tsuji was thrust into an age when Japanese society was still largely stratified and before the country's disastrous defeat in World War II – and the U.S. occupation that followed – brought this system to an end. Yamanashi is landlocked and largely mountainous, home to the country's highest and most revered mountain, Mount Fuji. To the east and south lie the prosperous cities of Tokyo and Yokohama. Without access to the sea, though, the prefecture was isolated as a production center. The poor quality of its land made rice cultivation difficult. To produce anything in Yamanashi, an old adage goes, you have to be either strong or clever.

The strong worked the land to produce silk, fruit and other prized items, the theory being that if you were going to sweat all day working rough land, you might as well grow something expensive. Yamanashi's finest also earned a reputation as excellent bodyguards, thanks to their good conditioning working the land and their loyal disposition.

Some, it is said, took jobs in the underworld guarding mob bosses.

Other folks used their wits and became traders. Yamanashi is home to one of the three most well-known merchant groups in Japan, along with Osaka's salesman and the Omi Shonin peddlers in Shiga Prefecture, near Kyoto. As we will see later, Tsuji very much shares this Yamanashi heritage, unafraid to take chances and chart new ground, and unafraid to get up once he has been knocked down.

According to his autobiography[8], Tsuji's childhood was a broken one. He was born into a wealthy Yamanashi family that was part of the Saegusa clan that dates back at least five centuries[9]. His mother ran three *ryokan,* or traditional inns, in the capital city of Kofu. Tsuji wrote little about these operations, but suggested that the businesses were profitable and his mother's family was held in some esteem locally.

Oddly, his father figured little in his retelling of his family history. Tsuji is vague about what became of him, but implied that he never made much money.[10] He faded from view by the time Tsuji reached his early teens, by which time most accounts referred to Tsuji as an orphan.

Tsuji has a younger brother and a younger sister, but as the first child, he was treated like a prince. Japanese sons are often doted on and the hopes and aspirations of the entire family ride on their shoulders. With a father largely absent and a dominant maternal family history, Tsuji probably received even more attention than normal. Tsuji wrote that growing up, maids in his home catered to his every beck and call.

Despite living such a relatively luxurious childhood, Tsuji was largely isolated as a kid. He speaks of few friends and few pleasant memories. His mother, who he describes as strict but caring, preferred he played at home and only allowed him to visit the bookstore on his own. Longing for friendship, he would tell his mother he was going to the bookstore and then make a detour to play traditional Japanese card games with the neighborhood kids.

By his own account, Tsuji was lonely and shy, hard pressed to forge meaningful relationships. But two events stick out in his memory. One teacher asked him to bring things to school to donate to the poor. Tsuji brought rice and old clothing and helped distribute the goods to the poor. Another time, Tsuji found some trading cards, and gave them to another boy. The smile on the boy's face taught Tsuji that giving things to people, even if the gifts are small and have little intrinsic value, was a good way to win friends. "I don't remember how I felt at the time, but I got a strong impression, 'I can please people if I give things to them,'" he wrote.[11]

LIFE TURNED UPSIDE DOWN

The cocoon where Tsuji lived for the first 13 years of his life dissolved when his mother died. His father faded from the picture with her death. Orphans in Japan, like elsewhere, never have it easy. Often they are thrust on relatives who resent the obligation and lash out at the kids they have been left to protect. Other times they are singled out and bullied or, worse, left alone. Since the lineage system in Japan is built around the primacy of the male heir, orphans lack a birth father who can serve as a benefactor and guarantor, a stigma that is hard to overcome.

Matters did not improve when Tsuji went to live with his aunt. Already introverted, Tsuji wilted under her tirades and criticism. He became gloomy as her bullying increased. Worse, World War II was raging which meant basic foods and other goods were in constant short supply. With few friends his own age, Tsuji felt as if he were a burden to the family. "I was treated as a good-for-nothing boy," Tsuji said. "I was scolded at so much that I became a gloomy boy who would always study my aunt's moods. Perhaps such painful and sad feelings were why I was attracted to the world of Greek mythology and had a strong longing for poetry and literature."[12]

In 1945, as the war winded down, Tsuji was faced with the possibility of being drafted. To avoid conscription, he entered Kiryu Technical College, which later became the engineering department of Gunma University in a neighboring prefecture north of Tokyo. There he learned to make things: sweeteners like dulcin and saccharine, soap and *shochu*, a Japanese gin-like alcohol. The ability to produce these and other essentials helped launch Tsuji's career as an entrepreneur.

With the end of the war, Tsuji, like the rest of the country, was freed from a destructive military dictatorship and years of oppression. The occupation troops commanded by Douglas MacArthur gave the country a new lease on life. Away from home at 17, Tsuji got a chance to start over at the end of the war.

The shortages immediately after the war, though, were legendary. The economy in shambles, everything from rice to paper to jobs was scarce.[13] Yet Tsuji proved to be an astute businessman, parlaying devastation into an opportunity, churning out soap and other goods in the school laboratories to sell on the black market. Though he glossed over the specifics, Tsuji suggested that he accumulated a small fortune through these sales. Despite its implications today, selling on the black market after the war was an ordinary, if not necessary, thing to do. In this, Tsuji proved resourceful.

He was unable to escape the critical eye of his aunt, however, who scolded him for selling goods on the sly and accused him of gangster ways. Now a young adult, Tsuji ignored her badgering and continued his business deals that allowed him to smoke and drink his way through college.

The party came to a halt when Tsuji, like many of his generation, contracted tuberculosis. Ill, he returned to his family's home in Kofu to recover, a process that took several months. Although he graduated from the chemical engineering department at Kiryu in 1947, his relatives, worried that he might return to his deviant ways, persuaded him to apply for a civil servant job so he could develop a respectable career as a bureaucrat. After passing a rigorous examination, he won a position with the government of Yamanashi Prefecture. Tsuji credits his older relatives with helping him gain entry into what was considered a hallowed world and a promising opportunity.

Tsuji was given a desk job, a position he called "the second adversity after my boyhood." Here, he calculated insurance fees and actuarial tables, a task that was torturously dull. Quick with numbers and seeing a chance to streamline a tedious process, he developed rate charts. The small innovation turned a month-long job into a project that lasted a few days. Having earned some free time, he amused himself by reading newspapers upside down and taking long breaks playing *pachinko*, a kind of vertical pinball game that is a popular pastime in Japan. His "bad" attitude was noted on his personnel evaluation and he was fired after less than a year.

Sensing his first job was coming to an end, Tsuji took an internal exam to join the commercial department as an instructor. He passed the test and was given a second chance as a teacher in the government. This, too, ended up boring Tsuji, who was eager for a job that would allow him to see more directly the fruits of his work. Whether through family connections or good fortune, Tsuji was asked by the governor, Hisashi Amano[14], to join his staff. Happily, he was given the task of promoting produce grown in Yamanashi. He set up offices in Tokyo, and his street smarts and enthusiasm caught the governor's eye.

PLOTTING AN ESCAPE

During this time – the 1950s – Tsuji married and his wife, Yasuko, gave birth to their only child, Kunihiko.[15] He barely mentions them throughout the rest of his autobiography; a not uncommon practice among Japanese businessmen who prefer to keep their personal lives private.

Back in the office, Tsuji still felt restless. The novelty of promoting vegetables and silk wore off even though he excelled at selling. Ultimately, he withered in his role, seemingly unable or unwilling to answer to a boss. So after 11 years in the government, Tsuji decided to quit. The audacity of this decision cannot be over emphasized. Though more stable than in the years immediately following the war, Japan was still struggling to get back on its feet. Jobs in the bureaucracy, with stable wages, fat pensions and post-retirement possibilities, were held in high esteem. Tossing that away while having a young child and wife to support must have been seen as mad.

In fact, Tsuji's boss did not accept his initial resignation, fearful of losing a valued worker and perhaps embarassed that a wayward former employee might reflect poorly on the governor. But he finally relented and agreed to let Tsuji leave on the condition he completed one last task. Facing reelection, the governor asked Tsuji to rent a plane, fly over the district and drop pamphlets that slandered the opponent. In return, Tsuji would be paid ¥350,000, equal to almost two years salary. Tsuji took the devil's deal but was saved at the last minute when the governor canceled the flight because all signs indicated he was going to win the election anyway. Tsuji burned the leaflets, returned the money and was allowed to resign at 32.

Tsuji's former bosses, eager to save face, also gave him a big push forward by investing in his first company, Yamanashi Silk Center Co., Ltd. The governor, the vice-governor and a handful of other bureaucrats invested ¥250,000 in the outfit. Tsuji added his pension from the government and personal savings to bring the total amount of invested capital to ¥1 million, a substantial amount those days. Thus, his career as an entrepreneur began in earnest in August 1960.[16]

THE YAMANASHI SILK CENTER

Despite the auspicious start, Tsuji lived precariously like many young companies. Early on, a client defaulted on ¥5 million ($40,000) in obligations, pushing the company to the verge of bankruptcy. To bounce back, Tsuji and his workers hit the road, selling their silk goods in open-air markets in front of public baths, which were central meeting places in many towns. In time, the company absorbed the losses, allowing Tsuji some room in 1962 to expand beyond silk into rubber beach sandals. Eager to distinguish his otherwise ordinary product, Tsuji embellished the sandals by fixing a small flower onto them. The "oriental sandals" attracted attention and the company soon received orders from overseas. Tsuji did not miss the message: By tweaking the design, he could turn an everyday item into a branded one and boost sales. So, he repeated the process with wallets, slippers and other goods, this time adding strawberry designs to them. "If you attach added value or design to the product, they sell in a completely different way," he explained.[17]

Emboldened by his discovery, Tsuji added cherries to his lineup when the mini-boom for strawberry designs faded. They were a flop, leaving Tsuji to learn another early lesson: Not all items in a category work well, whether it be fruits, animals or colors. Still, strawberries would remain a staple of Sanrio's marketing for many years to come. In his search for something more original – or in today's parlance, something with more "value added" – Tsuji commissioned well-known cartoonists like Ado Mizumori to draw characters for him. He took these and stuck them on coffee cups, plates and other pottery, a process he would later recreate thousands of times with Hello Kitty.

But Tsuji was bothered by what he perceived to be a major flaw in the arrangement: he had to pay the artists royalties and did not own the rights to their works. "If we could have our own original characters, maybe we could develop a new set of businesses with the copyrights," Tsuji said.[18] These might produce the "golden eggs" that would generate a steady stream of profits well into the future. Tsuji realized that unlike patents, which protect business processes and products for 15 years and are often not renewable, copyrights are protected for at least 50 years (and sometimes twice as long) after the death of the author. They can also be applied more easily across borders. To take advantage of this, Tsuji would need to build his own in-house design team that could churn out these characters, something he began to do in the mid-1960s.

The decade was an explosive one for Japan, when the economy was expanding at about 10% a year. With some wealth under its belt after World War II, Japan was opening to the world. Tokyo hosted the Summer Olympic games in 1964; capital controls were being lifted to allow for smoother investment overseas and jet airplanes made it easier to travel abroad. Japan's exporters were also making a name for themselves overseas with transistor radios, televisions and automobiles. Foreign cultures and styles – movies, clothing, music, art – were seeping into Japan, helping crack some of the insularity that long characterized the country.

Like many Japanese businessmen, Tsuji was keenly focused on what was going on overseas. In the character-goods industry, there was no place better than America or, more specifically, Hollywood. One of his lifelong dreams – never realized – was to meet Walt Disney. (He didn't visit America until 1969, after Disney died.) Tsuji was also a fan of Charles Schulz, the creator of the Peanuts comic strip, who he met in 1970. He eventually won the license to sell and market goods featuring Schulz's most famous character, the beagle, Snoopy.

He also sought and received advice from J.C. Hall, the founder and president of Hallmark greeting cards.[19] To his surprise, Tsuji discovered that other than greeting cards – which Tsuji had already moved into – the character merchandising business in the U.S. was still quite undeveloped. Disney had a Mickey Mouse clock, but it was not a mass-market product. The days of Warner Brothers shops and other retail outlets were still decades away. Disney, it seemed, was more interested in movies, television shows and theme parks.

With a team of designers, relationships with famous Japanese artists and a business driven almost entirely by the merchandising of its characters, Tsuji wanted to know what American companies received in royalties. He learned that there were no formal arrangements and decisions were made on a case-by-case basis, a rather lax set-up, he thought, given the scale of the businesses involved. He also learned that retail shops normally pay 10% per item sold while wholesalers returned a 3% royalty.

Tsuji's other contacts in the U.S. proved instructional. In 1966, he won the rights to import Mattel's Barbie doll, now the world's best-selling toy. Despite its popularity in America, Japan was not quite ready for the dolls. They were expensive because the dollar-yen rate was still fixed at 360. Japanese toy makers also quickly pumped out similar dolls more tailored to Japanese tastes. Tsuji derisively called these rivals "copy cats," but the result was the same: Sales of Barbie fizzled and Tsuji ended up losing ¥700 million ($5.8 million).

Tsuji also imported Hallmark greeting cards, something closer to his product line. However, he quickly learned that while Japanese are avid gift givers, the tradition of sending "Get Well" or "Mother's Day" cards is limited. (Even today, Japanese send just five to 10 greeting cards a year on average. Americans send about 25, while the British send about 50 per year.[20] The entire greetings-card market in Japan is still many times smaller than in the U.S.)

Another problem was that though the Japanese have a tradition of sending postcards at New Year's (*nengajo*) and in the summer (*shochimi mae*), they are rarely sent at other times. More importantly, the Post Office dominates this business, printing millions of pre-stamped postcards a year.

There were other problems. Since Tsuji imported the cards directly from Hallmark, most of them included pictures of babies with blue eyes, blond hair and other non-Asian features. Needless to say, the reception drew a less than enthusiastic response.

With sales going nowhere, Tsuji sold the license to import Hallmark cards to a printing company after just two years. However, he was forced to keep paying royalties to the

American company because he had signed a seven-year deal. Through this setback, though, Tsuji developed a vision of his company based on "social communication" where small gifts could be used to build friendships. He took his idea to Hall. The dean of the greeting-card business approved, but told Tsuji that each gift should come with a message; in other words, a gift with a card attached. The advice, perhaps self-serving considering that it could benefit Hall's business, made sense to Tsuji – the gift and card were the right combination to convey a message of friendship.

The trick was to find a good balance between quality and price. Expensive gifts have several potential pitfalls. The receiver might feel obligated to buy something of equal value in return, an awkward position for someone without the means. Or they might feel they are being bribed, particularly in a business setting. Pricey gifts may also appear pretentious, and expose the giver as a show-off. A cheap gift, on the other hand, might lead to just as many questions. The receiver might ask, "Is this all I'm worth?"

So Tsuji settled on something in the ¥300 to ¥500 range ($2.50 to $4.15). This price was also within reach of school kids, especially girls, who were more likely to swap gifts with their friends. It also fit in with a line of products like notebooks, pens and handbags that students were bound to buy. Tsuji took care not simply to plaster his cartoon characters on existing products, and instead tried to create original items. The formula worked, and has been expanded over the years to include more than 20,000 products. To keep its line fresh, the company introduces 600 new products a month and phases out the same number.

WHAT'S IN A NAME?

As Tsuji's product lines expanded through the 1960s, so did his ambitions. In 1969, he opened his first retail outlet overseas, the "Strawberry Shop," in San Francisco. Two years later, he repeated the concept in Tokyo's Shinjuku ward when he opened his first "Gift Gate" shop, a store that became a chain. As the company grew, Tsuji realized its name, the Yamanashi Silk Center, was no longer relevant and a stumbling block with audiences overseas.

Choosing a new moniker, though, was not easy. Tsuji wanted something simple and memorable. At the same time, the name should sound foreign and have a deeper meaning, yet not be insulting to non-Japanese. Tsuji was careful to not use words with sounds that could offend some groups. A casual student of history and a man with grand thoughts, he also reckoned that three of the world's oldest civilizations – the Babylonians, the Egyptians and the Chinese – were born near rivers, the Tigris, the Nile and the Yellow River. "San" is also the romanization of the word for "three" in Chinese and Japanese, while "Rio" means river in Spanish. So Tsuji settled on "Sanrio." In April 1973, the company was officially re-established using this name.

The new label also helped Tsuji distance the company from its earliest roots. One by one, Tsuji bought back the shares from the original investors, his co-workers from the Yamanashi government. Most of them were not interested in the shares anyway, because Sanrio was still an unlisted concern. Others were hard up for cash. Tsuji ended up buying back all of their shares, which by his calculations, would have netted ¥2.5 billion ($21 million) had they been sold on the market.[21]

In the meantime, Tsuji continued to expand his lineup of characters. The most famous, of course, was Hello Kitty, which was created in September 1974. The development of the cat will be discussed later, but it's fair to say that this one character, out of the more than 400 Sanrio designers have churned out, has changed the course of the company and of Tsuji's life. Indeed, the cat gave Tsuji the platform to pursue his global ambitions and to dabble in the arts, a pursuit he seemed to crave.

TSUJI GOES TO HOLLYWOOD

By the late 1970s, Hello Kitty was a modest success in Japan
and overseas. As the economy expanded, so did the character-
goods market and the amount of disposable income Japanese
had in their pockets for small gifts, cards and other items. By
most standards, Sanrio had "made it" and even won a listing
on the prestigious first section of the Tokyo Stock Exchange
in 1982, where the company remains today. Tsuji had expanded
into other media, including in 1973, a magazine called *Shi to
Meruhen* (*Poetry and Fairytales*). Two years later, Sanrio
launched the *Strawberry Shimbun*, a news magazine devoted
to Sanrio characters and specially designed for younger readers.
In 1976, Sanrio started to license its characters to other
companies.

In between, in 1974, Tsuji set up a subsidiary called Sanrio
Communications, Inc. in Los Angeles to produce films and
distribute Sanrio products in North America. The company's
first formal foray overseas was bold for several reasons, most
crucially because Tsuji had no experience in the film industry.
Driven by naivete or ego, he went straight to Hollywood
under the assumption he could go head-to-head against the
likes of Disney and Warner Brothers. It turned out to be an
expensive project lasting over a decade that produced more
than two-dozen films, most achieving little commercial success.
Although hard-core animation fans still enjoy the films, many
in Sanrio questioned the money-losing effort.[22]

"We produced a lot of films, but none were successful,"
said Etsuo Iida, executive vice president of Sanrio Inc., and
one of the first employees to be sent to California. "We were
not prepared to make money, so it was a mistake to get into
it. But [Tsuji] wanted to challenge himself because it helps
him express his creativity. From our point of view as a
business, it was not valuable. But from his point of view, he
did something valuable." Money aside, Tsuji was driven by
a fascination with Disney's *Fantasia*, which he had seen as

a child.[23] Wanting to produce a Japanese version along the same lines, he set about making animated fantasies, the first one, *Chiisana Jumbo (Little Jumbo)*.

The Sanrio-produced films came in various shapes and sizes. Tsuji tried his hand at scriptwriting on several occasions, including the 108-minute animated feature called *Syrius no Densetsu*, or the *Legend of Syrius*, released in 1981. Four years later, Tsuji wrote *Yosei Florence* (Fairy Florence), a slightly shorter animation that was distributed in the U.S. In other cases, Tsuji recruited top Japanese talent. At least two films were based on the works of Osamu Tezuka, the dean of postwar Japanese animation and the creator of the *Astro Boy* cartoons.

Sanrio Inc. did not limit itself to animation, producing action comedies, stage shows and documentaries. Tsuji's film productions also recruited big U.S. stars. One animated feature, *The Mice Family's Wonderful Journey (Oyaro Nezumi no Fushingina Tabi)*, included Sally Kellerman, Peter Ustinov and Cloris Leachman in key roles. Other films featured Katherine Hepburn and Burl Ives, while Sanrio's version of the *Nutcracker Fantasy*, released in 1979, included Eva Gabor, Melissa Gilbert, Dick Van Patten and Roddy McDowell.

Some of the films eventually made their way into home videos, and many were distributed in the U.S. as well as Japan. In 1980, Tsuji also opened the Sanrio Theater in Matsudo City on the outskirts of Tokyo to help promote Sanrio's films. The theater is still in operation today.

Despite Tsuji's efforts to expand the company's repertoire of creative talent, the film he is best remembered for is a documentary, *Who are the Debolts and Where Did They Get 19 Kids?*. Produced in 1977, the 72-minute film won the Academy Award for best documentary in 1978, making Tsuji the first and only Japanese producer to win the award. Directed by John Korty and made in conjunction with Charles Schulz Associates, the film profiles Robert and Dorothy Debolt and their 19 children, 14 of who were adopted. The kids came from different ethnic backgrounds and several were physically challenged. Narrated by Sidney Walker, the film looks at their lives in a lighthearted but thoughtful way. The film was a natural for Tsuji to back financially since he is a self-proclaimed orphan with dark memories of childhood.

Though his artistic works from that era barely register a reaction in Hollywood these days, Tsuji is proud of his award and knows that, even indirectly, it has opened doors for him and the company. At the end of one media interview nearly a quarter-century later, he made a show of having the golden Oscar ushered into the room and plunked down on the table in front of the reporters.[24]

But overall, the experiment in Tinsel Town generated far more losses than profits. Tsuji's almost one-dimensional – some say unrealistic – focus there would also presage other money-losing ventures, the most controversial of which is the Sanrio Puroland theme park.

THEME PARK ADVENTURE

Opened in December 1990 in Tama City, about a one-hour train ride from downtown Tokyo, Puroland was a lightning rod for debate from the outset. At its crudest, the park was seen as a bald attempt to mimic the success of Disney and Disneyland, albeit with a twist because the park is indoors. The park was also viewed as a testament to Tsuji's pretensions and self-indulgence borne in the late 1980s, when Japan's stock market was nearing its peak and money was cheap. The cost overruns and bloated final price tag of ¥70 billion ($600 million) dragged down Sanrio's balance sheets for years and is still being dealt with.[25] In September 2001, after years of losses, Sanrio unveiled a plan to overhaul the finances of three of its subsidiaries, including Sanrio Puroland Co., operator of the park, through debt-forgiveness plans and capital injections.

Cost was not the only factor. Critics felt the park was too far from Tokyo for most families to reach. At the time, Tama City was a relatively new suburban town that requires an express train ride from downtown. Others felt the park had too few rides (in fact, only one) to compete with Disneyland, which draws legions of visitors in search of thrills. Still others said an indoor park is too stifling and claustrophobic.

Tsuji, a strong-willed individualist, has fended off opposition, although he has admitted some of these problems. But the criticisms made him work harder to turn the park into a success. He visits the park almost every weekend, mingling with parents and kids, egging people on to dance, selling lottery tickets for prizes and making sure everything is operating properly. He plays court jester and king at once, a clown with kids and a commander towards employees.

To Tsuji, the park is a natural extension of his character-goods business, a place to showcase Hello Kitty and other characters, to bring them alive on stage and in dance revues, and allow young children to interact with these life-size cartoons. "I had been thinking for some time to have an experimental field for the coming age of live entertainment and to accumulate know-how about it," Tsuji said. "Honestly speaking, it was regrettable that Puroland has been belittled as an 'expensive box' without software."[26]

Tsuji's vision, in many ways ahead of its time, was undone by several critical blunders. To build and run the park, Tsuji set up Sanrio Communication World Co. (SCW) and installed his nephew, Yuichi Nishiguchi, as president.[27] Though Nishiguchi was an advisor at Sanrio, he apparently had trouble dealing with the flock of architects, designers and bankers brought in to build the park. The subsidiaries' payroll eventually ballooned to 2,500 workers, twice as large as the parent company. About 300 designers were hired from the American design firm, Landmark Entertainment Group, while others came from Disney and Universal Studios.

Tsuji stood by his nephew despite the rising costs – until just before opening day. That's when Tsuji learned that Nishiguchi had put together a show that included characters he had created, and gave only bit parts to Sanrio characters. Why Nishiguchi did not understand that Puroland was designed to be a platform for Sanrio characters is unclear. It is also unclear why Tsuji, who is normally fastidious about the use of his characters and rarely cedes decision-making control, did not monitor his grand project. Things got worse. Rather than use the proceeds from the park to help pay SCW's formidable debts, the money was rolled into fixed-term savings accounts. SCW eventually had to borrow even more money to meet its obligations. Compounding matters, the company ended up selling tickets in packages that left customers with more than they could use in a day.

In early 1991, with Sanrio about to complete an outdoor park in Oita prefecture called Harmonyland, Tsuji wrestled back control of SCW, pushing out Nishiguchi and others on loan from Sanrio's main banks. He also redesigned the ticket packages and shows in the park, and halved the subsidiary's payroll.

The troubled start cast a pall over the park, which ran up further deficits as the economy slowed through the 1990s. However, the revival of Hello Kitty midway through the decade sparked renewed interest in the park. In 2001, Puroland drew 1.38 million visitors, down 8% from 2000. Yet, 10% of the park's visitors are from overseas, a higher ratio than Tokyo Disneyland; according to Sanrio. About 80% of the visitors are also "repeaters" there for a second or third time. The average family of four drops ¥30,000 ($250) at the park, not bad in a recession.[28] "The prices are so high in Tokyo" that Puroland is a relative bargain, said Kazuhiro Manabe, a public relations officer for Sanrio Puroland.[29] "It's close to the train station, so it's easy for moms to bring their kids to the park without poppa."

Sanrio has also done an ingenious job weaving together a series of stage shows, dance contests and other events under one roof, not to mention many chances to drop money on

Sanrio products. Take the main event of the day, the Illumina Parade, Puroland's equivalent of a walk down Main Street in Disneyland. In just 20 minutes, kids and their parents are introduced to dozens of Sanrio characters, led by Hello Kitty. Trapeze artists, jokers and ballet dancers swirl around the "Wisdom Tree" built into the center of the German-style town square. Chinese acrobats on unicycles jump rope. Others do complicated back flips. The display is part fantasy, part circus, part Las Vegas stage show.

Despite his wealth and age, Tsuji still gets genuinely excited at the park. He eggs on the crowd to compete in singing contests, one of his recent innovations. "Sanrio thought it would be good to have an adult competition, not just for the kids," Tsuji said.[30] "If you don't dance, then you can't live. It's fine for Kitty to dance, too. Pokemon, Garfield – they don't dance."

Tsuji uses Puroland and its patrons as a kind of in-house market research laboratory. "He likes to hear from customers directly," said Puroland's Manabe.[31] Like many Japanese companies, Sanrio prefers to rely on intuition and first-hand experience rather than asking market-research firms and advertising agencies to survey strangers and customers for their opinions. "The customers know best," Tsuji said.[32] For example, through his frequent visits to the park, Tsuji noticed that fathers accompanying their kids looked increasingly bored. So Tsuji asked the dancers' outfits be made to reveal more of their legs and backsides. "If the dancers are not sexy, fathers won't come to see the show," Tsuji said.[33] "Recently, even grandfathers are showing up. We can't do dirty shows or show breasts, but we can show t-backs."

A MAN IN FULL

Tsuji's frankness and bluster are characteristic of a man sure of himself and his opinions. Like other company founders, Tsuji leads with his vitality and bluntness. When he enters a room, energy swirls his way. He walks quickly, speaks rapidly and directs conversations. After more than four decades atop Sanrio, Tsuji is comfortable in his role; he does not equivocate. "He's not a typical company president," said Manabe. "You can read him," a reference to his openness and the clarity of his goals.

Although Tsuji enjoys – and perhaps needs – to be the center of attention, there is nothing smug about him. He drives his own car to Puroland on the weekends and fawns over children there with a genuine fondness. He wears ordinary suits, combs his still-black hair neatly and keeps scrupulously neat. Were he not leading Sanrio, Tsuji could pass for an ordinary salary man. Inside Sanrio, Tsuji is known as "poppa" or "senior," the latter to distinguish him from his son, Kunihiko. Tsuji's own office is on the top floor of Sanrio's Tokyo headquarters and is full of stuffed dolls and other paraphernalia, plus a table full of handmade cards given to him by Sanrio employees. Yet restless, Tsuji spends most of his day walking from department to department, swinging through the legal team, consulting with the finance group or the designers downstairs. No detail, it seems, is too small for Tsuji to focus on, employees say, adding that he sometimes has difficulty stepping back.

"'Senior' has a passion in business," said Iida, Sanrio Inc.'s executive vice president.[34] "That's how he attracts people." At the same time, "he is not arrogant. His head is lower. He is willing to come to down to others' levels."

Iida first met Tsuji in the mid-1970s while he was a banker with one of Sanrio's main lenders. When his boss was seconded to Sanrio, Iida was asked to join him. Having studied in the U.S., Iida was sent to California to help Sanrio start its North American operations. Though Iida had little knowledge of Sanrio or the character-goods business, he was impressed with Tsuji when they met for the first time at the Beverly Wilshire Hotel in Los Angeles. "I knocked on the door and he opened the door standing in his underwear," recalled Iida.

"He said, 'Please take a seat,' and went back to his morning chores. I was surprised since the president usually wears a necktie. That changed my image of the company and him. He is as he is. He's no fake."[35]

While Tsuji scores high points for his honesty and energy, he does have his darker moments. Tsuji wrote openly about the stress of steering Sanrio through the first half of the 1990s, when the company's stock collapsed, sales turned south and several key investments soured. Aware that his job required that he at least appear confident, Tsuji internalized most of his stress, although the doubts about his ability and the company's future deepened.

"For a company leader, there is nothing more terrifying than to lose confidence," Tsuji said. "I couldn't show such misery to anyone. I tried to pretend to be fully confident, but inside myself, I was always shrieking, 'It's so hard, so painful.'"[36]

As the stress intensified, Tsuji said he considered suicide. "I couldn't sleep without sleeping pills," Tsuji wrote. "I was psychologically cornered to that extent and suffered loneliness that I had no one to consult with."[37]

In addition to Sanrio's financial problems, Tsuji was also weighed down by the everyday stress that accumulates after years leading a company. Tsuji is keenly aware that his character-goods business is built as much on trust as good design. That means Sanrio must keep a squeaky-clean image or risk alienating parents who want their kids surrounded by wholesome images.

"I have to take care of my image," Tsuji said.[38] "If I went to Soapland [a Japanese massage parlor] and someone took a picture of me there, it would provoke a scandal."

Years under a microscope, mounting losses and a stale market had compounded to depress Tsuji. But the clouds lifted in 1995 when he went to the hospital to have some lumps in his abdomen examined. The doctors found a potentially malignant polyp in his colon that required surgery.

The life-threatening condition broke the dark spell hanging over Tsuji. "Once I came to learn about my illness," he wrote, "my desire to live became stronger. In fact, after I came out of the hospital, I have never felt like 'I want to die,' however hard and painful things are."[39]

ROLLING THE DICE

Tsuji's recovery coincided with Hello Kitty's revival in the latter half of the 1990s. In this way, the cartoon cat saved Tsuji as much as the doctors and fate did. But Sanrio still faced problems. In fact, Tsuji's approval of some investment schemes, compounded by the popping of the asset-inflated stock market of the 1980s, led critics to wonder whether Sanrio was making money despite itself.

However, the roots of the problem go back decades. Tsuji has used stock trading to supplement Sanrio's operating profits for years. During Japan's long climb, this strategy worked well. Like many investors in the 1980s, Tsuji was also emboldened by the Bank of Japan's decision to lower interest rates and keep them there for several years. The central bank cut rates to 2.5% to offset the rising yen, a decision made in the aftermath of the Plaza Accord of 1985 between G-7 countries. The bank's cheap-money policy invited investors to buy real estate, stocks and other assets. The market soared and commercial land prices more than quadrupled. That encouraged yet more investment by people borrowing based on the collateral of their inflated real estate.

Tsuji, already an avid trader, did well during the 1980s, when Japan's stock market soared to its all-time peak. For several years during the decade, Sanrio's profits earned from trading equities matched or exceeded the company's operating income. With so much extra cash pouring in, Tsuji felt justified re-investing the money into projects like Puroland and producing films.

Tsuji and Sanrio, along with thousands of other companies, also invested in *"tokkin"* funds, or monetary trusts sold by insurance companies and trust banks. Investors used the funds to trade securities without taking unrealized gains on the stocks. By moving the stock into these monetary funds or fund trusts, they could trade the shares like derivatives without booking a profit on the original shares. At the end of fiscal year 1990, in March 1991, Sanrio had ¥96.9 billion ($808 million) in the *tokkin* funds and another ¥75.8 billion in stocks.[40]

The pot of money grew while prices rose. But when the market soured, the value of these derivatives, not to mention the underlying securities, plummeted. Compounding matters, disclosure on these accounts was poor, so investors were unable to get a full picture of the losses.

These investments came back to haunt Sanrio when Japan's stock market started its long slide on the first day of trading in 1990. Six months before, Sanrio's stock hit a record-high ¥9,040. Since Tsuji was an avowed believer in stocks and had as much as 40% of the company's assets in the funds, investors ended up punishing Sanrio's shares. The company's stock plunged 93% to ¥640 just two years after hitting its peak in mid-1990. "Shareholders felt penalized by Tsuji's securities hobby," said one analyst at an American brokerage.[41]

As Japan's bear market wore on during the 1990s, Sanrio's losses snowballed. Tsuji was reluctant to sell the funds because he would have to realize the losses. Yet in the four years from 1994, Sanrio accumulated losses of more than $400 million.[42] In 1998, with the market sinking to post-bubble lows, Tsuji, under the advice of his bankers', started selling some of the *tokkin* funds and using the money to pay Sanrio's debts.

The losses, though, overwhelmed Sanrio's balance sheet. The company lost money for four straight years through 1998, preventing Sanrio from paying dividends, a major embarrassment in corporate Japan.

"It was not that I was totally unaware of the signs of danger," Tsuji said. "I thought I had reasonable measures to cope with possible failure, but the *tokkin* funds ... generated a large amount of losses and eventually ate up Sanrio's profits. After all, the rapid deflation in assets that followed the bubble far exceeded my prediction. In that sense, my failure was enormous."[43]

Sanrio's retreat from the *tokkin* funds coincided with Hello Kitty's revival in Japan, which led to two years of profits in 1999 and 2000. Sanrio's stock also jumped above ¥6,000, still one-third below its record high, but six times more than its 1998 price. The company started paying dividends again and accelerating the write-off of its debts.

The turnaround, though, did not mean the company abandoned stocks altogether. In fact, Sanrio's financial team continued to invest about ¥37 billion ($308 million), about 20% of the company's assets.[44] As the stock market sank to near two-decade lows in 2001, the company took a bath on the downturn in technology shares like NTT DoCoMo, Ricoh and others. The losses helped push Sanrio back into the red, as it lost a net ¥2.67 billion ($22.3 million) in the fiscal year ending in March 2001. The company's stock portfolio declined ¥400 million ($3.3 million) during the period. Fiscal year 2001 was no better, with the company losing ¥5.1 billion on its stock investments. "It's a very big minus," when stock swings affect the earnings of companies like Sanrio, said Hiroshi Motoki, senior vice president of Alliance Capital Asset Management. "It's unpredictable and a terrible use of shareholders' money."[45]

For years, Tsuji was unrepentant. "I don't think that stock investments were a mistake at all," he has said on several occasions. "The executives of companies listed on the first section of the Tokyo Stock Exchange who madly invested in stocks, land and paintings until recently, all of a sudden started saying, 'the investment was a mistake, we will go back to our main business.' I was quite astonished. If a stock company denies stock trading, it denies itself."[46]

But as Japan's economic malaise deepened and the stock market sank yet again, Tsuji threw in the towel in October 2002.

At a news conference, he announced that Sanrio Ltd. would likely lose a net ¥13.2 billion ($110 million) – not a ¥2 billion profit as originally forecast – in the six months ending Sept. 30, 2002. The culprit was the stock market. The company lost ¥1.4 billion selling securities and would write down the value of its stock portfolio to the tune of ¥8.3 billion yen ($69.2 million).

"The outlook for the stock market just isn't getting brighter," Tsuji told reporters,[47] adding that the company would gradually sell off its holdings and close its fund management division.

Ironically, though he owns 3.9 million shares, or 5.0% of the company, Tsuji says he never sells Sanrio's stock, lest the profits distract him. "Sometimes, I'm called a billionaire, but I have never sold my shares before or after listing Sanrio," Tsuji said. "What I fear is a situation in which I would probably play around and lose the original purpose of investing, once I got a lot of money."[48]

GREENER FIELDS

Zapped by stock losses and slowing sales at home, where Sanrio sells almost 90% of its goods, Tsuji has stepped up efforts overseas, where growth remains robust. Under the guidance of Tsuji's son, Kunihiko, Sanrio has expanded into more than three-dozen countries. Tsuji, though, planted the seeds of the expansion more than a quarter of a century ago, when he established Sanrio Inc. in California. Sanrio now operates 44 shops in U.S. and sells at 3,000 stores.

In 1980, Sanrio opened a branch office in West Germany, forming Sanrio G.m.b.H. in Hamburg three years later. A subsidiary was added in 1987 and Sanrio Far East Co. followed in 1990.

Although Sanrio products are now sold globally, their closest affinity has been in Asia outside Japan, something that will be discussed later. Tsuji set up subsidiaries in Taipei in 1992 and Hong Kong in 1994.

Out of total sales of ¥114 billion in fiscal 2001, overseas sales made up 13%, almost three times more than a decade before.

But Sanrio relies on overseas for more than just sales. Half of Sanrio's products are made by outside suppliers overseas, Tsuji dubbed this a "fab-less" production process, a reference to the lack of machinery and factories. "It is better to work with contractors, particularly now that Asian production lines have grown competitive in quality," said Tsuji.[49] The products are then licensed to franchises in return for royalties and profit-sharing revenue. A stroll through the gift shop at Puroland shows how high up the retail food chain Sanrio has climbed. Hello Kitty and other Sanrio characters are found on Parker pens, Shiseido cosmetics and Samsonite luggage.

While Tsuji is happy with this arrangement, he is careful to acknowledge the growing backlash toward products made outside Japan. So each year, Sanrio holds "Made in Japan" campaigns with towels, stationery and other domestically produced goods. It's an acknowledgement that as global as Sanrio has become, ultimately, it is a Japanese company that must continue to win hearts at home.

ENDNOTES

[1] Shintaro Tsuji, *Kore ga Sanrio no Himitsu Desu* (The Secrets of Sanrio), trans. Chieko Tsuneoka (Tokyo: Fusosha, 2002), 109.

[2] Shintaro Tsuji, Founder and President, Sanrio Ltd., personal interview, Aug. 1, 2002.

[3] Ibid.

[4] Character Goods Databank White Paper, 2002, Tokyo.

[5] Mary Roach, "Cute Inc.," www.wired.com, Dec. 1999, <http://www.wired.com/wired archive/7.12/cute.html?pg=1&topic=&topic_set=>.

[6] Bill Gates' offer to buy the Hello Kitty brand has turned into near-legend. According to Kazuhide Yoneyama, an assistant manager in the general affairs department at Sanrio said, Gates and Tsuji have never met. Rather, a Microsoft board member relayed a message to Tsuji about Gates' offer. Tsuji has confirmed the offer. Microsoft denies any knowledge of these discussions, and his reply.

[7] Tsuji, personal interview, May 19, 2002.

[8] Tsuji's autobiography is as much memoir as it is company history. Although he discusses his childhood, his jobs in government and the birth and growth of Sanrio, it also includes chapters on how to succeed in business and his philosophy of interacting with employees. He also includes tips on how to win at the racetrack and other seemingly off the wall sidebars.

[9] Tsuji, 112.

[10] Ibid., 114.

[11] Ibid., 112-113.

[12] Ibid., 112.

[13] For a detailed description of conditions in postwar Japan, see *"Embracing Defeat: Japan in the Wake of World War II,"* by John Dower. W.W. Norton & Company, 1999.

[14] Tsuji does not say whether Gov. Amano was a family friend, but it is entirely possible that, given his family's wealth, someone in Tsuji's family could have had access to the top levels of government. Regardless, the governor appeared to take a liking to young Tsuji, at least according to Tsuji's retelling of it in his autobiography.

[15] Kunihiko Tsuji now works in Sanrio as a head of overseas operations and is widely considered next in line when his father steps down.

[16] In later chapters of his autobiography, Tsuji talks in detail of how to become a company president. He mocks those who marry daughters of company presidents or those who were born into wealthy families, ignorning the fact that his own company received a significant boost at a crucial early stage from his former bosses.

[17] Tsuji, 93.

[18] Tsuji, personal interview, Aug. 1, 2002.

[19] Joyce C. Hall (1891-1982) founded not only Hallmark Cards, but was one of the fathers of the modern greetings-card industry. In many ways, Tsuji was his Japanese kindred spirit because, like Hall, he preaches happiness. Tsuji also learned from Hall – a fellow entrepreneur – many techniques to market that happiness in the form of products. Tsuji still speaks enthusiastically about Hall and his generosity.

[20] Etsuo Iida, executive vice president Sanrio Inc., personal interview, July 26, 2002.

[21] Tsuji, 132.

[22] Iida, personal interview, July 26, 2002. Iida was one of the first Japanese managers sent by Sanrio to the U.S. in the 1970s. Iida originally worked for a Japanese bank, which was one of Sanrio's main lenders. When his boss left the bank to join Sanrio, he recruited Iida.

[23] http://www.pelleas.net/hm/25/shtml.

[24] Tsuji, personal interview, Aug. 1, 2002.

[25] Yoshinori Omura, *Nihon Keizai Shimbun*, June 8, 1991,"Indoor Theme Park a Real-Life Headache: Puroland Shocks Shake Sanrio."

[26] Tsuji., 16-17.

[27] Omura, *Nikkei Weekly*, June 8, 1991.

[28] Figures provided by Kazuhiro Manabe, Public Relations at Sanrio Puroland.

[29] Manabe, personal interview, May 19, 2002.

[30] Tsuji, personal interview, May 19, 2002.

[31] Manabe, personal interview, May 19, 2002.

[32] Tsuji, 18.

[33] Tsuji, personal interview, May 19, 2002.

[34] Iida, personal interview, July 26, 2002.

[35] Ibid.

[36] Tsuji, 12.

[37] Tsuji, 13.

[38] Tsuji, personal interview, Aug. 1, 2002.

[39] Tsuji, 14.

[40] Sanrio Chief Sees Danger in Stock Prices, *The Nikkei Weekly*, Sept. 7, 1991, 14.

[41] Cesar Bacani and Mutsuko Murakami, *Asiaweek*, March 19, 1999, Pretty in Pink: Japan's Sanrio is riding the Hello Kitty craze. How can it make the good times last?

[42] Ibid.

[43] Tsuji, 23.

[44] Eric Bellman, Heard in Asia: Hello Kitty has a Sweet Purr, but her Master Likes to Bet, *The Asian Wall St. Journal*, July 15, 2002.

[45] Ibid.

[46] Tsuji, 23.

[47] Sanrio to End Stock Investing *Nihon Keizai Shimbun*, Oct. 2, 2002.

[48] Tsuji, 68.

[49] Cesar Bacani and Mutsuko Murakami, *Asiaweek*, March 19, 1999.

Chapter 3

The Cat Comes Alive

Japan is a nation of trains. Hundreds of subway and commuter lines crisscross this narrow country, including the famous *shinkansen* bullet trains that rocket millions of passengers up and down the main island of Honshu. The center of all this activity is Tokyo Station, one of the busiest depots in the world. Every day, 1.8 million people file through its multilevel buildings with their brick facade.

Like any main thoroughfare, Tokyo Station is filled with coffee shops, snack bars, convenience stores and restaurants. There are also dozens of stands selling *ekiben*, or Japanese boxed lunches filled with savory specialties like baked fish, stewed vegetables and pickled sushi. Nearby, too, are stands selling gifts for busy commuters and travelers to bring home to their families.

These stalls lining the middle hallway of the station sell boxes of cookies, cakes and other sweets wrapped and ready to go for the salaryman on the run. Stumped for a gift idea? How about a box of green tea *manju* filled with sweet bean paste, or chocolates shaped like the Tokyo Tower, an Eiffel-looking structure that doubles as the capital's main television transmitter.

59

But most of the merchandise are targeted at kids, especially girls. Many of the cookies and cakes are cut in the shapes of popular children's characters, so-called *ningyoyaki* that includes the faces of Doraemon, a blue cat-like beast who loves *dorayaki* sweet cakes. Indisputably, though, the biggest sellers are the cookies stamped with the face of a demure cat, Hello Kitty.

The stalls inside Tokyo Station run by a Japanese confectioner, Sanki, do a booming business selling Kitty cakes, Kitty cookies and Kitty chocolates. A box of red bean paste-filled Kitty heads costs ¥630. A dozen custard cream Kitty cookies will set you back ¥1,050. In an average month, the stands there sell ¥70 million ($560,000) of sweets. During the holidays, especially *O-Bon* in August, when people who live in the city take their families back to their rural homes, the shops sell a whopping ¥120 million in Kitty treats that go for between $5 and $15 a box.[1] This amazing retail sensation – these are just small cakes, after all – is a testament not only to Hello Kitty's wild popularity, but the savvy marketing of her owners at Sanrio Ltd. Of course, clever products placed strategically in prime retail space are a sure-fire formula for making millions. But Sanrio has also ensured that the cakes' quality is equal if not better in taste and texture than the next best product. For if the Kitty cakes don't get kids squirming for more, parents are sure to view them as gimmicks and potential repeat business will be lost.

"Basically, we first think about how to make good products," said Akito Sasaki, a manager at Sanrio's domestic licensing and special sales department. "We realize that if we make bad candy, people won't buy it again."[2]

Sanrio's grasp of the need to package quality with ingenuity extends far beyond sweets. There are thousands of Hello Kitty products, each designed, produced and distributed by Sanrio, or licensed to other companies who pay Sanrio between 3% and 10% as a royalty. The range of Hello Kitty goods is so massive that it requires more than 200 designers, product planners and lawyers to produce, maintain and protect. There are Hello Kitty toys, of course, and stationery, kitchen goods, home appliances and personal computers. There's a 34-diamond watch (list price: $30,000) with Hello Kitty staring from the face, sequined evening bags (a big hit with movie stars in Hollywood) and mobile phones in all the latest designs. Hello Kitty has also gone native. She's dressed in 130 "regional" outfits that reflect the history and customs of Japan's 47 prefectures. Need a lift? Buy a Hello Kitty surfboard, bicycle or a compact car built by Daihatsu.

The list goes on so long that some critics say Sanrio is spreading Kitty too thin. By sticking her white face on everything from toasters to vibrators, the company is eroding her uniqueness and making it expensive for die-hard fans to collect Kitty goods. And by selling her image under license so frequently, the company also risks losing control of the way its products are sold, a particular problem outside Japan, where the meaning and use of characters are interpreted differently. A sharper, more coordinated approach to managing the Hello Kitty brand is essential to ensure she keeps thriving, they say.

Still, taken together, Hello Kitty generates about $500 million a year in revenue for Sanrio, about half the company's annual sales, and billions more for the companies that lease her image. Hello Kitty is the most lucrative character in Japan, and one of the top five money-earners worldwide. But unlike other licensed products, Hello Kitty did not begin life as a television or movie cartoon. So how did this simple cat reach such financial heights? Who are the people behind her perpetual incarnations and what's their strategy? And who came up with her frightfully simple design – that white face, black button eyes, yellow nose and six whiskers? Read on to find out.

AT A CROSSROADS

Sanrio opened its doors as the Yamanashi Silk Center in 1960, and though the company had some minor hits during its first few years, its unlikely rise to stardom really started with Hello Kitty 14 years later. Like in other parts of the entertainment business, the genesis of the cat's popularity is both entirely random and perfectly obvious in hindsight. By the time Kitty came along, the company had already pumped out some characters and had started to build a small in-house design team. President Shintaro Tsuji had learned in some crude form how to license character goods that his designers generated and ones that he distributed under license from others, including Hallmark Greeting Cards and Charles Schulz's Snoopy. By the early 1970s, Tsuji was starting to build a name for Sanrio in Japan's tiny character-goods market.

But Sanrio was at the crossroads. Though it was growing steadily and was profitable, the company was still quite small with just a few hundred employees, versus about 1,000 now. In the year before Hello Kitty was born, 1973, Sanrio earned a modest $1.05 million profit on sales of $14.9 million. Sales were just 1/50th of its 2002 revenues. The company was almost a decade away from listing on the Tokyo Stock Exchange, a big measure of a corporation's "arrival" in Japan's business world. Back then, the company's offices were still tucked away in the Gotanda district, a nondescript neighborhood of Tokyo's inner city. Sanrio still had little overseas presence.

The company was dwarfed by the real might of Japan, manufacturing. Japan in the 1970s was all about "hard" industries like steel, shipbuilding and automobiles. Japan's bureaucrats had successfully built a national business model that was geared toward serving increasingly global giants like Toshiba, Toyota and Nippon Steel, makers of the televisions and cars that put Japan on the map with consumers in the U.S., and beyond. The country's largest banks funneled Japan's massive pool of savings toward these huge conglomerates, especially those that competed overseas and earned precious dollars that inflated the country's trade surplus, the island nation's piggybank.

With the government, banks and manufacturers in full embrace and the economy rising phoenix-like out of the ashes of World War II, it is easy to see why a small design company barely warranted attention. Cute dolls and colorful lunchboxes were nice, but they were clearly accessories to the industries that kept Japanese factories humming and the country's growing workforce fully employed. Cartoon characters were the kind of softer merchandise that the industrial titans dismissed as kid stuff.

Japanese cartoons were not high on the agenda overseas, either. America had *Mickey Mouse* and *Bugs Bunny*. Disneyland was a top attraction in California and a new, bigger Disney World was opening in Florida. Animation and comic books were big businesses in America already, so there was little need for input from foreign countries, with rare exceptions. Few at the time saw Japan as a producer of worthy entertainment. About the only media commodities that had made the journey across the Pacific were *Godzilla* and the cartoon, *Speed Racer*. Even then, the monster movie was altered to fit American tastes. First released in Japan in 1954, some scenes were deleted and new scenes with Raymond Burr, later of *Perry Mason* fame, were added for release in the U.S. two years later. Though the film was a runaway hit in Japan, it barely made a ripple in the U.S. and was appreciated more for its kitsch value.

Far from the mainstream, Tsuji, in his own scattershot way, was adapting his small company to take advantage of the licensing and character-goods industry, as well as Japan's fast-changing sensibilities, especially those of women and kids. He knew, for instance, that licensed goods, if protected legally and not overexposed, could provide a steady stream of income. He also understood that cute sold – and sold well – if it was designed with delicacy. Unlike American cartoons, which tend to be bold, full of aggressive colors and sharp lines, Sanrio's characters are more subtle, with rounder features, more pastel colors and a kind of coziness that strike a chord in Japan. Hello Kitty typifies this style.

Still, Tsuji was not enthralled with Kitty when an in-house designer, Yuko Shimizu, showed him the first drafts of the cat. Fortunately for him, he allowed the product to come to market. Kitty's success reaffirms what many professionals will tell you: Breakthroughs seem to happen when you least expect them, and the development of a hit product is one-tenth skill and nine-tenths luck. There are so many variables at work that anyone who says he "knew" his product was going to take off is suspect. Tsuji, who has operated much of his company by instinct and rarely employs methodical market research, was no different.

Think of all the things that need to be in place for a product to take off. Timing, of course, is crucial. If Sanrio had introduced Kitty when the first *Star Wars* movie came out and kids were gaga for Jedi knights and light sabers, she probably would have been decapitated and tossed into the trash heap. Instead, she hit the market just as Snoopy was tugging at Japan's purse strings. Animals were the rage with kids in the 1970s, and not just the Age of Aquarius Unicorn patches that girls wore on their bell-bottom jeans. American television shows, many of which were exported to Japan, fed kids a steady diet of anthropomorphic animal stars, including Lassie, Flipper, the friendly dolphin and Gentle Ben. In a sign of their lasting popularity, some of these shows are still rerun on Japanese cable television.

Animals were just as dominant in the cartoon world and Tsuji was smart enough to set aside his strawberries and cherries and tap into this new fad. His big coup in the late 1960s was to win the rights, along with two other companies, to sell Snoopy goods under license in Japan. In fact, Hello Kitty's current designer, Yuko Yamaguchi, learned of Sanrio in the 1970s because she was a fan of Snoopy, not Hello Kitty.

Of course, the character-goods market in Japan was not and is not a zero sum game. Take a walk through Shibuya or another trendy Tokyo neighborhood and you'll see kids with several different characters plastered on their tee shirts, mobile phones and backpacks. A pink Kitty cellular phone might include a chain with Pokemon, Doraemon or even Austin Powers as an accoutrement. In many ways, this menage of characters makes it harder for companies to catch people's attention. Tsuji, however, found a formula by positioning the cat in the warm and cuddly part of the market inhabited by young girls.

This emerging market for "cute" things grew out of Japan's newfound wealth. As the economy expanded and Japan's manufacturing might increased, many of the country's creature comforts, like cozy homes and down-to-earth cities, were destroyed. In their place, skyscrapers and impersonal apartment blocks that would make an East German proud sprouted higher.

Long, mind-numbing commutes took the fun out of work and, increasingly, women became servants to their salarymen husbands who brought home the bacon but rarely saw their kids. Stuck in new, remote bedroom communities, women wanted comfort, and Hello Kitty, with her soft features and homespun story, was just the kind of nurturing creature to help them escape the hostile, industrialized urban world.

Kitty quickly struck a chord. The year she was released, 1974, Sanrio's sales grew almost threefold from the year before. Between 1974 and 1977, sales grew sevenfold and profits grew tenfold. Tsuji realized the fleeting nature of the character-goods business, so worked quickly to cash in on his success. He shifted resources within Sanrio to capitalize on his hit, expanding the product line in Japan and taking Kitty overseas, decades before Super Mario and Pokemon became worldwide phenomena.

Managing his property with a long-term view has proven trickier. With the benefit of decades of hindsight, Tsuji said he understood that Hello Kitty could not be expanded too fast because consumers would burn out on the brand.[3] But when you've got a winning product, it's hard to hold yourself back. So Sanrio ramped up production and started licensing its big hit. By the end of the 1970s, sales growth started to level off. However, Tsuji found out that Kitty had the right mix of cuteness and cuddliness to make a comeback. Revenue resumed its steady climb through the 1980s (although at a slower rate), when Sanrio was involved in movies, amusement parks and the stock market. In 1982, when Sanrio listed its shares on the Tokyo Stock Exchange, sales had jumped to $406 million. Despite occasional hiccups in sales growth, Tsuji stuck with the Hello Kitty brand. "Any character has good times and bad times," Tsuji acknowledged in his autobiography. "So it was with Kitty-chan."[4]

Tsuji didn't give up on Kitty, but he certainly endured wild swings in sales and profits, thanks to his Hollywood venture and theme-park construction. The investments, however, put Kitty back on the map with consumers and sales jumped again at the beginning of the 1990s, before dropping off quickly, when the economy fell back into recession.

These swings suggest to some that Sanrio had never found a proper formula to ensure that Kitty grows steadily. Instead, it has been forced to capitalize on the capriciousness of Hello Kitty's fans, who turn hot and cold to the cat. This, critics argue, is partly because Kitty lacks a coherent storyline that keeps kids rooted to the character week after week. (Sanrio has helped produce only one television series, "Kitty's Paradise," a children's cartoon that has aired on TV Tokyo since 1993, but it has never reached the heights of, say, the Pokemon series.) Her status as a symbol – and a commercial one at that – means people flock to her and abandon her with lightning speed.

Kitty's Second Coming, in the mid-1990s is a perfect example. The cat had gone into a slumber for several years and sales dipped. They surged again as Japan came out of recession and Kitty's original fans started raising families of their own and bought the products for their kids. Sanrio also focused more heavily on marketing products that adults would appreciate. But the real trigger for Kitty's rocketing revival came in 1997, thanks to pop diva Tomomi Kahara, who blurted out that she loved Kitty on the well-known television show, "Utaban."[5] "Within days sales in our outlets had nearly doubled," said Sanrio marketing manager, Ko Takahashi. "Since then we have been actively searching for every niche Kitty has yet to fill."

Every niche indeed. Kahara's fortuitous appearance ushered in some fat years, and Sanrio did not waste any time unleashing another blitzkrieg of products on the market. The company now designs, produces and sells 6,000 Hello Kitty products. Another 16,000 Hello Kitty products are also sold under license. In many ways, Konami, Nintendo, Sega and other Japanese character-goods companies have Sanrio to thank for expanding a market that they have since joined.

"PINK MAKES YOU HAPPY"

Legends are funny things. They are often based on kernels of truth and then twisted into grander stories as the years go by. By any standard, the discovery of Hello Kitty is a sliver in the character-goods industry timeline, but her story is shrouded in various myths nonetheless. In his autobiography and other published accounts of Kitty's birth, Tsuji omits key facts and is intentionally vague, at times professing all-knowing insight, and at others, appearing awestruck about how she was first developed. Whatever his representation years later, it is clear that in the late 1960s, after the failure of his experiment with cherries and other designs, Tsuji knew that an in-house design team was crucial to the company's long-term success. At that time, Sanrio relied mainly on two famous cartoonists, Ado Mizumori and Takashi Yanase to create new characters. Unfortunately for Tsuji, the artists held the copyrights to their work and Sanrio had to pay them commissions.

This, Tsuji knew, made it hard for him to shape the direction of his product line and boost profit margins. "If we could have our own original characters, maybe we could develop a new set of businesses with the copyrights," Tsuji wrote. "So I set up a design section in the company and started to recruit designers who might produce the 'golden eggs' of the future."[6]

It all sounds very casual now: Hire a few art students, sit them down with some sketching paper and pencils and get them to draw some cartoon characters and fruit. In fact, that's largely what happened. Starting in the late 1960s, Sanrio's half dozen or so in-house designers took the drawings that Mizumori and Yanase produced, as well as others, and refashioned them so they could be plastered on small accessories and ceramics. In a few years though, the designers grew frustrated by the limits of their work and complained to Tsuji, who encouraged them to come up with their own characters. "Perhaps animals are good," Tsuji told his small team, taking a hint from the imported greetings cards he sold.[7] But which animals were best?

According to Tsuji, dogs are the most popular animals in Japan, with cats and bears close behind. Squirrels, chicks, ducks and rabbits also have followings, but only with toddlers. Wild animals like elephants, lions and giraffes score points with young kids, and whales and dolphins have their groupies, too. Birds, on the other hand, are seen as fluttery ("neurotic," in Tsuji's words) except for owls and penguins, which are coy or cute. Insects are definitely out, given their association as pests. In the end, Tsuji chose the cat, partly because Snoopy and Winnie the Pooh were already a popular dog and bear, and partly because Sanrio already had a dog and bear in its stable.

Color was another issue. Brown and green, both earthy colors, are natural but drab. Kids don't get excited about brown. Tsuji considered blue, which, he said, made a "humorous and sporty impression." But it is also a masculine color so more suited to boys. Besides, Doraemon, the pastry-eating cat popularized in comic books and on television, had already made his debut and he's a light shade of blue. Red, however, was extremely popular in combination with white and went well with other light colors like yellow, something that might attract girls. "Red-oriented colors symbolize warmth, little girls, little animals and love, so is most suited for characters," Tsuji said.[8]

Designers agree with Tsuji's interpretation. "Kids respond to certain colors and shapes and they have a basic understanding of textures and patterns," said Bob Eggleton, an internationally known science-fiction artist and designer who has worked extensively in Japan.[9] "Primary colors work well with characters. In particular, red is a strong color and, of course, red and white equal pink, which is very feminine. If you focus on red and white side by side you see two colors, but when you blur past them, you subconsciously see pink."

Some go even deeper. "At the time kids are born, red has the biggest impact," said Yuko Yamaguchi, who has been in charge of Kitty's design since 1980.[10] "But pink is the cutest colour and has the most feeling. Pink makes you happy."

"NOT-TOO-BAD IMPRESSION"

Kitty was not the first character Sanrio's newly emboldened designers came up with. Looking at some of the early creations, you can see elements of what eventually became Hello Kitty. For example, Sanrio designer Hiroko Suzuki created Patty, who was later paired with Jimmy to become a boy-girl team. Patty has braided pigtails while Jimmy has his hands in his pockets. Like Kitty, both have huge heads as large as their bodies, no mouths and large dots for eyes. Suzuki, a graduate of a design school on the northern island of Hokkaido, continued to ignore Tsuji's plea for animal designs, and instead drew apples. In one incarnation, the apple was split in two and an English caption read, "Love is to Share." Tsuji was not particularly impressed with Suzuki's work, saying it was "too complicated," but the "Love is" series that grew out of this design became a big success.[11]

Around this time, another designer, Yuko Shimizu, began working on cats. A graduate of the prestigious Musashino Art University in Tokyo, Shimizu initially wanted to become a teacher. As one of Sanrio's original in-house artists, she had gone through a period of designing fruit. She was a big fan of cats, so took well to Tsuji's appeal for animal designs.

While reading *Through the Looking Glass* by Lewis Carroll, she was taken with the cats in the book and thought they were "cute." So she played with her designs a bit, turning the cat sideways to show its profile, then turning it again to show it looking straight ahead. She took them to Tsuji, who was initially noncommital. She went back to the drawing board, continuing to work on cats, though few ever seemed to meet with Tsuji's approval including, it turned out, Hello Kitty.

By the time Shimizu finished tinkering, Hello Kitty's design was in place. She had a white head twice as large as her body, a yellow button nose, six whiskers, no mouth and two dots for eyes, which looked right at you. Kitty was dressed in a blue coverall with a red ribbon by her left ear, slightly askew. Her small figure sat sideways in a red field. On one side of her was a bottle of milk with a straw, and on the other, a small bowl with a red fish inside. Despite its visual appeal, Tsuji had his doubts about whether Hello Kitty would catch on. "To tell you the truth, I only had a 'not too bad' impression of it when I first saw the drawing." "At that time, I never imagined it would be Sanrio's biggest character. The arrival of Kitty-chan was a major step forward to my dream for the copyright business."[12]

BORN IN LONDON

Shimizu, a fan of Alice in Wonderland, wanted to build a fairytale around the Hello Kitty character to humanize her and make her more feminine. So she gave Kitty a "real" name,

Kitty White. Part of an archetypical British family, Kitty, according to her life story written by Sanrio, was born in London on November 1, 1974. George and Mary White are Kitty's papa and mama, and her twin sister, Mimmy, looks identical except she wears a yellow bow over her right ear. Anthony and Margaret White were added as grandparents later. The Whites live in a brick house a half-hour outside London, with a green lawn and plenty of friends nearby.[13]

Kitty and Mimmy are in the third grade and Kitty, we are told, likes to travel, listen to music, read and eat "yummy" cookies that Mimmy bakes. She is also quite the socialite with oodles of friends, including bears, rabbits, sheep, monkeys and mice, though the majority of them were created by Kitty's third designer, Yuko Yamaguchi, because, as Hello Kitty likes to say, "you can never have too many friends." Her outgoing and kind-hearted nature makes it easy for Sanrio to introduce new characters into her storyline; however, while they are all cute, they are one-dimensional. We learn little about them except their dominant personality traits. A white rabbit named Cathy is considerate. Fifi, a lamb, is precocious. Tippy the bear is sweet and strong (and also has a secret crush on Kitty). It's as if these other characters are mirrors for Kitty to reflect the saccharine sweet ideals Tsuji wants Sanrio to promote.

Despite developing these additional characters, Hello Kitty's life is decidedly open-ended. She does not evolve or mature with her audience. In fact, though the trappings that surround Hello Kitty have become more complex, she remains locked in a kind of kindergarten fantasy where the deepest debate might be about whether to eat ice cream or cookies as a snack. "We work very hard to avoid things that would define the character," said Bruce Giuliano, vice president of the licensing division at Sanrio Inc. in Los Angeles.[14] "All of Sanrio's characters are very minimalist, at least from its back story, and they are also minimalist in a graphic sense. Hello Kitty contains very basic design elements and because of that minimalist design, it speaks to some very fundamental things about what kids identify with."

Though Giuliano admitted that this marketing strategy devoid of hard edges "may have been an accident," Sanrio realized long ago that it worked and has stuck to its formula. Hello Kitty is not a comic book with a story that progresses to keep readers interested. Instead, she is an icon that allows viewers to assign whatever meaning to her that they want, a character suitable not only for children, but for adults who may see Kitty as an escape back to childhood or a fashion statement. In this way, she is a character driven almost entirely by "feel" and serendipity. And by tweaking Kitty's design each year, Sanrio can keep her current with the latest styles. By adding characters to the mix, Kitty can be surrounded by props and new locations. In this way, Tsuji said, "Kitty-chan's success was never born by accident," but by design.

PASSING THE TORCH

Although Kitty was designed in 1974, the first Hello Kitty product was introduced to the world in 1975, when her sweet visage was plastered on both sides of a small clear vinyl coin purse. Above Kitty's head, just below the metals snaps, is the word "Hello!" in red letters. The small keepsake was designed for kids and cost 240 yen (less than $1 at the time). Sales took off and Sanrio released other products in short order. In most of the designs, Kitty is in a simple sitting pose and only the props around her. On other occasions, her clothes are different. In addition to stationery, Sanrio released dolls, toys and small appliances, like clocks. True fashion statements were still to come. Sales were strong, doubling in 1975 and again in 1976, when Sanrio licensed its first Hello Kitty products. Profits, too, hit 5.6 billion yen ($46.7 million) in 1977, a level not reached again for eight years.

It was during this time of rapid growth that Yuko Shimizu left Sanrio to get married and start her own family. So, in 1976, Setsuko Yonekubo took over as Kitty's second designer. She gave Kitty her first standing pose. In successive years, Yonekubo also put Kitty behind the wheel of a small propeller plane and riding on the back of a dolphin.

To cope with Kitty's newfound fame, Tsuji built a bigger design team. During the late 1970s, Sanrio was hiring more workers, including new designers. One of those was Yuko Yamaguchi, the woman who would become Hello Kitty's steward and soul mate for more than two decades. But in 1978, the straight-talking Yamaguchi was uninterested in furry animals. While studying at Joshibi University of Art and Design in Tokyo, Yamaguchi worked part-time at an advertising agency and wanted to design conceptual projects. But this was Japan in the 1970s, a time when men still ruled the workplace and where women were expected to serve tea, find a husband and leave the company. "When I was an art student, I wanted to work for an advertising agency, but in those days, Japan still hadn't introduced the equal opportunity law and a woman couldn't be an art director at an ad agency," Yamaguchi said a quarter century later.[15]

During her final year at design school, Yamaguchi heard of openings at Sanrio. She knew about the company because she frequently visited Sanrio's Gift Gate retail outlet in Shinjuku, a few minutes' train ride from her university. Though she recognized Hello Kitty, it was Snoopy that brought her to the store.

When Yamaguchi entered Sanrio in April of 1978, she never imagined she would become the caretaker of the world's most famous cartoon cat. Work at most design companies was extremely one-dimensional. Sanrio proved to be an exception. "I joined Sanrio not because I wanted to do character design, but because I wanted to explore my potential," Yamaguchi said. "Most of the companies [I visited] had already shaped their business into specific, narrow areas like developing or designing characters for stationery. But in the case of Sanrio, if you joined the company as a designer, you could get into any area, not just product design, but also things like Sanrio shop design or card design. Though the company wasn't as large as it is today, in the design section, there was an atmosphere that I could be doing anything in the future."[16]

Like all new employees, her first task at Sanrio was to take part in a worker-training program. Most Japanese companies have an initiation that takes new entrants through the rituals and routines in the office to shape them into company men and women. At larger companies, the programs can last up to two years, after which time workers present a report that managers use to evaluate their future role. Sanrio, though, was still small, so Yamaguchi was assigned to a project team with about 15 others who were supposed to come up with ideas for creating products that could be sold to adults.

The creation of the team, which was formed before Yamaguchi joined, showed that Tsuji understood, even in the 1970s, that selling just to kids would limit the company's potential growth. He knew if he could take some of the same characters and plaster them on goods to be sold to adults, he could charge more for them and broaden his lineup. In this way, he was ahead of his time and has used the strategy effectively, designing Hello Kitty products for older women and the young at heart, his so-called "high-target" audience.

About 18 months after Yamaguchi joined the project team, Yonekubo, Kitty's second designer, left Sanrio. Her departure coincided with a slowdown in interest in Kitty after the first three years of rapid growth. So Tsuji asked several designers to come up with new ideas for Kitty. Though the assignment was not a formal contest, Yamaguchi's design was selected as the winner. She put Kitty behind the keys of a blue grand piano. On top of the piano is a pink teakettle filled with red roses. Kitty is surrounded by Papa and Mama White and Mimmy - whose head barely reaches the edge of the piano. A couple of sixteenth notes float above, adding a whimsical feel to the picture.

It turned out Yamaguchi had unofficially auditioned for the position. Her winning design appeared in the *Strawberry Shimbun*, a newspaper that Sanrio published to give fans the latest news about the company's characters and new products. While Yamaguchi's design was not turned into any products, she was asked to become Hello Kitty's chief designer, a job she started in January 1980 and has held ever since. Less than two years in the company, still nursing dreams of a big career in advertising, Yamaguchi had mixed feelings about becoming caretaker of a decidedly juvenile character. "If I had joined Sanrio hoping to draw Kitty and was then actually able to do it, I would have felt extremely happy. But I feared that once you were appointed as the person to draw Hello Kitty, you wouldn't be able to draw other stuff, or that since Kitty was already a completed character, I wouldn't be free to design her as I wanted."[17]

Despite her misgivings, Yamaguchi soon realized that by working at Sanrio and taking on the task of designing Hello Kitty, her career could travel down many new avenues. She found working with a single character was not as limiting as she imagined. Unlike American companies, which often strictly regulate the size, shape and other characteristics of their cartoons, Sanrio was more liberal with its designers and allowed them, within certain boundaries, to experiment as they saw fit. "Take the example of Kitty's eyes," Yamaguchi said. "Sometimes she has smiling eyes or sleeping eyes or other times she is winking. Also, the size of her eyes is not defined down to the detail. It is not like the design is defined that precisely. You don't measure it with a ruler or anything like that."[18]

A DESIGN A YEAR

At first glance, Yamaguchi appears to be an unlikely steward for a pop icon like Kitty. With long, brown tinted hair cut square across the forehead, red lipstick and white nail polish, she looks more of an 1980s rock-and-roll groupie than the queen of cute. Despite her jarring appearance, Yamaguchi is extremely serious about her job, working long hours with her design staff of 40, plus the dozens of workers in the planning and marketing departments that crank out the thousands of products that keep Sanrio in business. Her most significant contribution, though, is coming up with an annual design for Hello Kitty that sets the tone for that year's products. Looking back more than 20 years, it's easy to see not only how Kitty evolved, but also how Yamaguchi made her the cutting edge of cute fashion.

In 1981, Yamaguchi put Kitty in a small red racecar with the letter "K" on the front door. The word "vroom..." waves below the car, as Kitty seems to be whistling while she drives. In 1983, Kitty is sipping a cup of hot cocoa against a gingham background with the words "What's New" above her right ear. Below her is the word "Pleasantime" (Sanrio's spelling) in red script letters. The use of English words is crucial in Japanese modern design. They not only accent the graphic design, but add an international flair, even if it makes no sense in English. So while "Pleasantime" is not a word, set in a picture of Kitty sipping cocoa, it connotes intimacy, comfort and safety, with a dash of Western culture thrown in.

While the trappings around Kitty became more complex, Kitty remained true to her minimalist self. "I get the impression that American characters strike an active, dynamic pose and their limbs are long. Whereas Japanese characters, including old characters, are in a stationary state, just standing there, and their limbs are not that long, with no neck and no mouth," Yamaguchi said.[19]

Though red and pink are used most frequently, Yamaguchi has branched out. In 1985, Kitty sits against a deep blue background as she reads a story to a small stuffed bear. The year before, Sanrio experimented with photography, sitting a stuffed Kitty at a table eating an ice cream parfait. In 1988, Kitty sits against a red and black tartan background. In all of these cases, Yamaguchi searches for what's fashionable not only with young kids, but with their parents who buy them the Hello Kitty stationery, clothes and toys. "I read all sorts of magazines to see what's in style. I especially like [the sophisticated fashion magazine] *So-en*," she explained. "I watch a lot of television dramas to keep up with the latest trends. For example, I noticed there's a revival of the shows that were popular in the 1980s. Watching these shows, I wondered if 1980s fashion would make a comeback, too. I watch various TV shows that are popular with our target audiences. For example, I try to figure out what young kids are into by watching *Sesame Street.*"

Yamaguchi is mindful that parents decide what young kids wear, so she considers their tastes as well. These women also buy Kitty for themselves. And the market for kids is segmented, so kids in grade school will need different designs from the kids in junior high school. "Of course, the basic design for Kitty is the same," Yamaguchi said. "But in recent years, we cater to specific age groups and make designs accordingly."

THE FANS SPEAK

Yamaguchi also listens to Hello Kitty's fans. She receives about half a dozen letters a day from people as young as three years old as well as grandmothers. Some letters Yamaguchi responds to, but most are fans writing for advice about their love life. Some treat Kitty like a pop star – someone they can dream about and carry on fantasy relationships with, she said.

Others are more practical, including one letter that led directly to one of Kitty's more controversial designs. In the late 1980s, a Japanese high school student wrote to Yamaguchi and said her friends and parents were pushing her to stop collecting Hello Kitty because, they said, it was for young girls, not teenagers. So the fan asked Yamaguchi to come up with a design that high school girls could collect. Yamaguchi, taking a hint from the monochrome fashion boom at the time, drew a white silhouette of Kitty against a black background, something that would match the kids' handbags and clothes. "In order to use black, I felt I should make the design extremely simple but had a graphic arts feel to the detailing," Yamaguchi said. "Such a simple design would suit high school students."

Despite its groundbreaking features, the design was not a hit with the president. Tsuji was more concerned with whether the design was cute than making a fashion statement. "President Tsuji basically only says 'it's cute' or 'it's not cute,'" Yamaguchi said. "When he is shown a design he doesn't like, he will ask 'would it sell or not?'"

Despite Tsuji's personal skepticism with the monochrome Kitty, he gave Yamaguchi a lot of room to operate, allowing her to develop a relationship with the cat. Her busy day of meetings and appointments starts around 9:30, and she is involved in many discussions about characters other than Kitty. Yamaguchi tries to set aside time after 6 p.m. to work exclusively on the cat.

To keep herself focused and her designs fresh, Yamaguchi turned Kitty into a kind of alter ego. As the years passed and Kitty became larger than life, Yamaguchi changed the way she perceived the character and took a more supervisory role.

"In the early days, I felt that Hello Kitty was like my other self," said Yamaguchi. "Back then, I tended to have Kitty wear the clothes I wanted to wear and do the things I wanted to do. But my perception has changed over the years. Now I think about how to promote her and in what way I should create her. Rather than her being my other self, I feel like I am Kitty's manager or producer. If Kitty is the star, I am in a position to produce her, so to speak."

By developing a persona for the cat and treating her like a public figure, it is easier to imagine what fashions will add to her fame and popularity, said Yamaguchi. And by objectifying Kitty, it makes it easier to redesign her.

Changes that may seem minor to the untrained eye sometimes have a significant impact. Some market watchers say Hello Kitty's revival really started in the mid-1990s when Yamaguchi put her on a pink background and replaced the bow with a five-leafed flower in 1995. Sanrio at the time was pushing pink for its "high-target products," those more expensive items aimed at young adults rather than kids. Yamaguchi realized pink would be hot when she went shopping in Harajuku, a Tokyo mecca for young kids. She saw a set of watches with black, red, pink and white straps. She noticed that the pink ones sold best, so she started drawing Kitty with more pink.

Yamaguchi also ditched Kitty's ribbon in favor of a flower because she imagined that if she was tired of ribbons, Kitty must be too. There were no angry letters, so Yamaguchi took it as a sign that fans accepted the change. Yamaguchi has made other additions, including giving Kitty a sun tan when she appears on some summer goods.

Designs, however, are not enough. Yamaguchi must coordinate with Sanrio's marketing, planning and licensing departments responsible for packaging these designs into a multitude of products that make up the bulk of the company's income.

(NO) SEX, DRUGS OR ALCOHOL

After almost three decades, Hello Kitty remains one of the most popular and profitable characters in Japan.[20] With few movies or media products to promote its golden cat, however, Sanrio churns out hundreds of new products every month to keep kids and their parents coming back for more. Since Sanrio earns the bulk of its profits through the sales and licensing of its products, the company must keep an open mind about what constitutes a worthwhile product. At the same time, it must guard against expanding into product categories that might sully the pure image Kitty and her friends are meant to promote.

Tsuji is practical about this, giving his designers and product managers ample room to work. Rules, such as they are, mirror his own preferences. "Sanrio does not have precise rules like 'You should not do this or that,' and we don't try to follow abstract and noble mottoes," he said. "Detailed rules would alienate flexible thinking and ideas, and I don't believe in reciting mottoes like mantras at morning meetings to heighten workers' morale."[21] In practice, this means that the marketing and planning departments are free to produce any product except those that involve or promote sex, drugs, smoking, hard alcohol and violence. "President Tsuji decides which goods he wants and doesn't want," said Masayo Hirose, assistant general manager of the product-planning department at Sanrio Co. "We don't make products that we think mothers would want to hide."[22] Anything else, she said, is in bounds.

Though many others in Sanrio echo this party line, the company has certainly tried to make a buck – when it can – off of sex appeal. There are Hello Kitty vibrators, for example, that are less than appropriate for tots. The master of Kitty himself, Tsuji, has also flaunted his own rules. At the Puroland theme park, he ordered the dancers to wear shorter skirts to show as much skin as possible. His intent: To make the shows sexy enough that dads and granddads would accompany their wives and kids to the park.

The product development team is divided into several groups: those that work on products Sanrio makes and sells, and those that they license to others. Another section handles the direct sales channels via the Vivitix retail chain and other store sales. A legal department polices the products once they hit the shelves. Another team works with Sanrio's subsidiaries in Europe, the U.S. and Asia to come up with products suitable for each region. Hello Kitty often makes up more than half of all products produced by these groups.

Sanrio's product-planning group is the heart of this operation. With more than 50 people, the team maintains a list of about 12,000 products on the market half of which are Hello Kitty. Each month, they come up with another 600 or so new items, half of them Hello Kitty and the other half a mixture of My Melody, Baby Cinnamon, Twin Stars, Patty and Jimmy and dozens of other Sanrio characters. Products are divided into three main categories: seasonal, everyday and promotional, depending on a product's lifecycle. Pens, staplers and other accessories, for example, are durable and for many seasons. Summer toys sell well only a few months each year. The design or packaging for certain snacks may last as long as a decade.

Within these categories, Sanrio divides products into five age brackets: babies, kids, juniors, teens and adults. One or several people may be in charge of seasonal goods for kids. The planning team also divides the year into three cycles during which each group comes up with a line of goods. As a rule of thumb, summer lines are developed between February to July. The autumn-winter line is produced between July and October, while the spring line comes together between October and December. Some goods, like baby bibs, can be sold year-round, so each list includes items rolled over from the previous season.

Like Yamaguchi, the planners must keep up on the latest trends and products. Often, salesmen are the best windows into what's hot since they visit the more-than-1,700 stores in Japan that sell Sanrio goods. (Thousands of other stores sell Hello Kitty goods, but they mostly buy them through third-party distributors, not Sanrio.) The product development and design groups have a dynamic relationship. Planners come up with a list of products they want to make, and Yamaguchi's department designs them for the producers. Storekeepers also request new items.

Since Sanrio spends very little on advertising, it must make products jump from the shelves. They also must gauge what customers are willing to pay for a product. Hello Kitty is a premium brand, so charging a bit more than the competition gives the products cache. But charging too much turns off customers. The products must also be well made or customers will complain. "Our working philosophy is good planning, good design and reasonable price," said Hirose of the product-planning department.[23]

With no manufacturing facilities of its own, Sanrio works with hundreds of vendors to produce its products. To ensure that these are well made, the company keeps tabs on the merchandising and quality. Sanrio has developed long relationships with its vendors; two-thirds of them have worked with Sanrio for more than 20 years.

LICENSING

The licensing department is structured much like the product-planning department, though it must deal with many more companies that want to sell Kitty. Within this department, workers look after toys, bags, clothing and accessories, candy and food, financial-related and miscellaneous products. Like in other groups, the workers are responsible for all Sanrio's products, not just Hello Kitty. With just 62 people, the department handles 21,000 products under license, 70%, or 16,000, of which are Hello Kitty. In all, Sanrio has licensing relationships with 520 companies in Japan and hundreds more through the company's subsidiaries overseas.[24]

Despite its size today, the licensing operation started almost by accident. After Sanrio started making Hello Kitty products in the mid-1970s, companies came knocking asking if they could make their own Kitty goods under license. Although the company signed contracts to distribute other companies' characters, like Snoopy, they had not yet worked the other way. So Sanrio quickly assembled a department to deal with the growing number of requests.

Now that Hello Kitty is well known, the company has changed the way it promotes its products. In years past, Sanrio would make samples and go from company to company to meet potential clients. But the company realized it was too costly to produce these samples, so in 1994, Sanrio ditched the system and instead worked the phones and used printed designs. The licensing department has since shrunk by one-quarter, sales have doubled and profits have tripled. In fiscal year 2001, the department earned ¥14 billion ($117 million) in pre-tax profits on sales of ¥44 billion yen ($367 million).[25]

SATURATION POINT

Thumbing through the hefty product catalog Sanrio distributes monthly, one gets a quick sense of the sheer variety of goods it handles. It also suggests that Kitty may be overexposed. In the early days, Kitty had focus: young girls. The company's first licensed product was a child's futon made by Nishikawa Sangyo. Morinaga, one of Japan's largest confectioners, made Kitty candy. This quickly spread to lunchboxes, pencils and pens and dolls.

These days, though, Hello Kitty is turning up everywhere. In the Gotanda neighborhood of Tokyo, Big Echo has opened a musical pantheon devoted to Kitty. This operator of a nationwide chain of karaoke shops has licensed the cat and decked out each room in pure Kitty. On a typical Friday night, dozens of twenty-somethings mill around the lobby with their dates, most wait more than half an hour to belt out Barry Manilow tunes in rooms with velvet Kitty wallpaper and sip beer from small glasses adorned with Kitty's face. Customer pay $8 an hour, less during weekdays and afternoons, for the privilege. This is the tip of the feline iceberg. Sanrio also has agreements with nearly two-dozen banks (mostly for credit cards and passbooks), a pool in Yamagata Prefecture, two ski slopes in Nagano, and even a Hello Kitty bowling alley in Okinawa. In addition, Sanrio works with 20 different electronics companies and has quickly moved into the cellular phone market. More than one million Japanese customers now have Kitty on their phones, paying between ¥100 (83 cents) and ¥400 a month for games that have Kitty in the starring role. KDDI, the country's second largest mobile phone carrier, has sold more than 100,000 Hello Kitty handsets since 2000.

Daihatsu even started making Kitty cars in 1996 and sold about 200 of these champagne pink compact cars per month in Japan before they were phased out in September 2002. "We originally called Toyota but they said no," said Sasaki of the licensing department. "Nissan said no, too. Mitsubishi Motors said yes, but would only make a fixed number. Suzuki only wanted to make a car with a male cartoon character. So we called Daihatsu." The biggest buyers of the cars, which are decked out with Kitty face on the doors, seats and other places inside, are young moms with daughters.

For high volume items, Sanrio generally charges a lower royalty of around 3%. For low volume products, the royalties can run as high as 8% or more. Contracts are usually for one year, but can last five years for service-related products, like credit cards. The company is paid based on the number of goods produced, not sold.

With services though, the company often negotiates one-time fees, annual payments or both, and often demands exclusive agreements. The overseas teams have their own calculations to make based on the markets they operate in. There is also a huge problem, especially in China, with companies overproducing goods but not paying Sanrio for everything they make.

Churning out thousands of Kitty goods and sticking her face on every conceivable consumable have their risks. "The most difficult thing is '*mannerism*,'" said Hirose of the product-planning department, using the Japanese play on the word "to imitate." Staying fresh, in other words, is not easy.

This has become increasingly difficult over the years, she said, because the company has produced so many goods already. In fact, some critics say Sanrio, in its drive to remain up-to-date and in people's face, has spread itself too thin and cheapened the brand. "In Sanrio, the priority is 'as long as it sells well,'" said Hidetoshi Iwabuchi, the managing director at United Media K.K., the Japanese subsidiary of the U.S. company that controls the rights to the Peanuts cartoon and characters. "It's not right to develop Kitty without limitation. She's too exposed in terms of merchandise and sales."[26]

The question of how Sanrio, with Tsuji at the helm, manages Hello Kitty's brand is crucial to the future of the company. Well into his 70s, Tsuji is nearing retirement. His son, Kunihiko, who runs Sanrio's overseas operations, is being groomed to take over the business. Like other companies, Sanrio is eager to expand overseas as a way to make up for slowing momentum at home.

ENDNOTES

[1] Akito Sasaki, manager, domestic licensing & special sales department, Sanrio Co., personal interview, Nov. 1, 2002.

[2] Ibid.

[3] Tsuji, personal interview, Aug. 1, 2002.

[4] Tsuji, 103.

[5] Alex Jordan, "Big In Japan: Hello Kitty!,"http://metropolis.japantoday.com/biginjapanarchive/234/biginjapaninc.html.

[6] Tsuji, 97.

[7] Tsuji, 98.

[8] Tsuji, 99.

[9] Bob Eggleton, personal interview, Sept. 30, 2002.

[10] Yuko Yamaguchi, designer, Sanrio Ltd., personal interview, Sept. 10, 2002.

[11] Masafumi Nishizawa, Sanrio Monogatari, (Tokyo: Sanrio, 1990), 50-51.

[12] Tsuji, 100.

[13] http://www.sanrio.co.jp/english/characters/w_chara/02.html.

[14] Bruce Giuliano, vice president of the licensing division at Sanrio Inc., personal interview, July 26, 2002.

[15] Yamaguchi, personal interview, Sept. 10, 2002.

[16] Ibid.

[17] Ibid.

[18] Ibid.

[19] Ibid.

[20] Character Databank, Tokyo, "Character Popularity Ranking" July 2002. Hello Kitty ranked #2 behind Winnie the Pooh among women, and #5 among men.

[21] Tsuji, 177.

[22] Masayo Hirose, personal interview, Oct. 2, 2002.

[23] Ibid.

[24] Sasaki, personal interview, Nov. 1, 2002.

[25] Ibid.

[26] Hidetoshi Iwabuchi, United Media K.K., personal interview, Oct. 2002.

Chapter 4

Kitty Goes Abroad

Carmel Li is your typical workaholic Hong Kong professional. Educated, fashion-conscious and upwardly mobile, she takes her job – and her free time – seriously. Like many Asian cities, Hong Kong is cramped, with millions of people packed into narrow streets and pencil-thin high-rises. Getting away often involves lots of work, assuming you have the energy. So when Li was in her mid-20s, the stress of her job as an assistant buyer at a big department store in the city started to prove too much. Working from eight in the morning until 11 at night, she barely had time for herself, especially if the boss took her and her office mates out for dinner.

Though she bought thousands of dollars of goods for her store, she had little time to shop for herself. During her occasional breaks in the morning, before work got too hectic, she started browsing to blow off steam, and it was then that she discovered a Sanrio store nearby. Since she didn't shop much, she had plenty of spare cash. So she started buying some Hello Kitty goods to add a stroke of whimsy to her otherwise frenetic day. First she bought some notepads, notebooks and a pencil holder for her desk. Then she added a flowerpot and a mouse for her computer. The floodgates opened when she bought things for her home: stuffed animals, a lamp, a pair of pajamas and some baskets. At 26, Li had become a full-fledged Kitty addict.

"I built my own Hello Kitty world at home in order to escape from the pressures of the outside world," Li mused.[1]

She had to go underground, though reluctantly, when she quit her job at the department store and moved to the marketing department at HSBC, one of Hong Kong's biggest and most prestigious banks. As cute as she is, Kitty didn't go over well with the stodgy, pinstriped bankers who were concerned about their image. Childish behavior was ground for censure. Anyway, Li was approaching 30 and about to get married, so would have to move apartment and lead a totally different lifestyle.

Instead of abandoning the cat entirely, Li found another way to feed her obsession: buying Kitty for her four-year old niece. Stickers, clothes, raincoats, candy, drawing books, you name it, and the little girl is now hooked, too. Li also bequeathed much of her Kitty collection to her. Still, every once in a while, Li gets the urge. When Sanrio launched a line of Kitty wedding products, she couldn't resist and bought a photo album for her wedding photos. "It's okay," she said, "it's a private item and others won't see it!"

Carmel Li's story is illustrative of the latest phase of Kitty's nearly 30 years on the scene. Not only is Kitty finding a growing audience among young adults, but she is also finding them outside Japan. Sanrio's mouthless feline is no longer the preserve of Japanese school kids and their lunch pails, but is a hot item in Hong Kong, Taiwan and throughout Asia, as well as the U.S. and, increasingly, Europe. Though Sanrio unleashed Kitty in America and Europe in the 1970s and 1980s, she really took off as a global phenomenon when Japan's Asian neighbors flocked to the cat in the 1990s, just as their economies were hitting their peaks.

Kitty's growing popularity worldwide – especially among adults – is testament to her wide appeal. Hello Kitty is available in more than 40 countries and the company, trying to offset slowing sales in Japan, is eager to develop these overseas markets.

Kitty, along with a wave of other Japanese characters, music, animated cartoons and comic books, are proving that America does not have a lock on globalizing its pop culture. In fact, in many ways, Japanese cultural exports resonate more deeply in Asia than American food, music and movies. Millions of teenagers in Hong Kong, Seoul and Bangkok covet the latest fashions from Tokyo, most of which never make it to New York.[2]

Japan is fast becoming a cultural superpower, replacing much of its industrial ambition with its soft-sell fashion, art and food. The country's influence overseas – whether it be Kitty, *manga* or J-Pop, as Japanese popular music is known – must be taken seriously, if only because so many people in so many places seem to like it. The scorn heaped upon Japanese pop culture – that it is shallow and derivative of Western culture – is largely irrelevant as a business proposition if it sells. In fact, some consider this superficiality an asset. Japan "has succeeded not only in balancing a flexible, absorptive, crowd-pleasing, shared culture with a more private, domestic one, but also in taking advantage of that balance to build an increasingly powerful global commercial force."[3]

Nothing is more representative of this trend than Kitty, the most purely commercial cultural export of them all. Like at home, Sanrio's subsidiaries offshore are churning out hundreds of new products, licensing her likeness to a wide array of manufacturers and service providers. Her growing power overseas comes at a crucial time for Sanrio. Sales have tapered off in Japan since hitting their peak in fiscal year 1998. Persistent deflation, falling wages and rising unemployment have pushed consumers to throttle back on spending, and Sanrio has felt the pinch. Sales fell 8.8% in fiscal year 2001, the third straight annual decline.

Sanrio is no innocent victim. The character-goods market in Japan, though worth a robust $16.7 billion (2 trillion yen),[4] is saturated and competition is intense. Sanrio has played its part, critics say, because it has relentlessly rolled out products to the point of overkill. Though Hello Kitty has soared to tremendous peaks of popularity, the company's strategy of blanketing the market with her image is leading to cute fatigue, as she falls in and out of fashion and becomes more disposable because of her overexposure.

Longer term, Sanrio, like most of corporate Japan, is wrestling with a demographic conundrum. The country is aging fast and the population of young people is shrinking. The number of 16-year-olds nationwide peaked in 1989 at about two million, during the height of the bubble economy. Since then, the size of this group – high-school kids who are also core Kitty fans – has fallen by about 500,000, or 25%. That means fewer high-school girls looking for Kitty cell phones, notebooks and other adornments.

So instead of being the icing on the cake, sales from overseas are now a crucial portion of Sanrio's business. Sanrio generates 16.5% of its revenue through exports and sales outside Japan, more than three times as much as in 1990 and 50% more than in the late 1990s. Sales in three of Sanrio's biggest overseas markets – Hong Kong, Taiwan and South Korea – grew 20-25% through the late 1990s and into the new century.[5] At the end of 2000, Sanrio was so encouraged by its reception overseas that it unveiled a bold plan to push into new markets. By 2005, the company wants to increase the number of foreign outlets it directly runs to 100 – a 150% increase – and boost sales from overseas by 66% to $210 million.[6] To that end, Sanrio opened its first store in Shanghai, in December 2002, and plans to open another 50 in China over the next three years.[7] Clearly, expanding into new markets overseas is one of the keys to Sanrio's long-term prospects.

KITTY BECOMES A GLOBETROTTING TIGER

Although Sanrio's expansion has kicked into overdrive, Kitty has been sold in Atlanta, Bonn and Caracas for decades, though hardly in large amounts. Selling overseas may sound run-of-the-mill in today's increasingly intertwined world, but back in the 1970s, it was unusual in Japan for a tiny service provider like Sanrio that was trying to sell products in markets where titans like Disney and Warner Brothers ruled.

Looking overseas, though, is a typical business strategy in Japan, an island nation with few resources.

Indeed, because of the dense web of wholesalers and retailers, the cost of doing business in Japan is often far more costly than in other major economies. This keeps large swathes of businesses operating, but also bilks consumers and stunts growth. It is a major reason why many of the country's largest manufacturers lose money on their sales in Japan.

To stay afloat, these companies rely on markets overseas, where the costs of producing and selling are lower and consumers are equally if not more ravenous. Japan's carmakers, for instance, earn about three-quarters of their profits offshore. Companies like Sony Corp. and Matsushita Electric Industrial Co. have similar profit profiles, and have also moved many of their factories offshore. These days, a stagnant home market makes selling overseas all the more important.

With the exception of a couple of airlines, hotel chains and department stores, few Japanese service providers operate overseas and then only in places frequented by Japanese tourists. The Takashimaya department store, for instance, has a shop on Fifth Avenue in New York and Japan Airlines flies you there. Contrast that with, say, the Hilton Hotel chain, McDonald's fast-food franchise or Toys 'R' Us stores, all American service providers that have expanded overseas and have strong, global brand names.

So by Japanese standards, Sanrio was ahead of its time. Tsuji realized early on that the center of the character-goods industry was in the U.S., and specifically the West Coast. Tsuji was egged on by Teruyuki "Terry" Ogisu, a former senior managing director at Sanrio who had a strong background in international business from his days working for Mitsui & Co., Japan's largest general trading company. To be taken seriously, they felt the company needed a presence in Los Angeles to rub shoulders with the Hollywood executives who developed the latest trends, had access to the best technology and collaborated on the most elaborate deals. Whether innocent or bold, Tsuji knew he had to be in America if he expected Sanrio to grow beyond its Japanese audience.

"He was stepping into a big market, but he didn't have the training; there was a certain amount of naivete involved," said Christine Yano, an associate professor of anthropology at the University of Hawaii who is studying global trends in the consumption of cute items. "For a lot of Japanese organizations, the whole process of business turns into something larger, more philosophical."[8]

Tsuji made his first links abroad in the late 1960s, when he started importing Hallmark Greetings cards and licensing Snoopy and other Peanuts characters. Soon after, he started to sell Sanrio's characters in San Francisco. Encouraged by the reception at that store, Tsuji opened the predecessor to Sanrio Inc. in Los Angeles in 1974, the company's first overseas office. The outfit also produced films. Two years later, after Hello Kitty had already taken root in Japan, Sanrio Inc. was established in San Jose to take over product development and distribution, years ahead of Japan's computer game makers and more than a decade before Nintendo, Bandai and others released Super Mario and Pokemon and other characters. In 1980, Sanrio established a toehold in Europe by opening a field office in Germany. Seven years later, the company did the same in South America, when it set up a subsidiary in Brazil.

Sanrio was also not shy about moving into other parts of Asia. Starting in 1990, as the Tiger economies of Hong Kong,

South Korea, Taiwan and Singapore were roaring, the company opened Sanrio Far East Co., a subsidiary that found cheap production outlets in China. Four years later came Sanrio Hong Kong Company, which was a sales subsidiary. The company now has offices in South Korea, too. To emphasize his commitment to the strategy, Tsuji put his son, Kunihiko, in charge of the day-to-day operations of the Hong Kong, Korean and other overseas subsidiaries.

However, the shift overseas came with hiccups. Despite Tsuji's aspirations, Sanrio's early years in America were far from fruitful. Tsuji pumped millions of dollars into money-losing movies that did little to promote Hello Kitty or other Sanrio characters. Though Sanrio characters are now sold in more than three-dozen countries, there was no grand acceptance in the early years. The portion of Sanrio's sales from overseas was only about 5% in 1990, a decade-and-a-half after the first overseas subsidiary in California opened.

For years the U.S. was Sanrio's biggest market outside Japan, making up 60% of overseas sales. But the numbers were small, and sales volatile. Sanrio Inc. introduced Kitty to Americans in 1976, two years after she was born. Sanrio produced a film featuring Kitty two years later, but the flick flopped. Then, a few years later, came the temperature-sensitive Kitty debacle. Sanrio introduced a doll called "Hello Color" that changed colors when you dunked her in a hot bath. It was a minor hit in Japan but sank like a torpedo in the States. It turned out Americans don't like piping hot baths and tepid water was not enough to make Kitty change colors. Colorless Kitty stacked up in the warehouse. The blunder indirectly contributed to Sanrio's closing its New York office and dismissing 40 employees in the late 1980s.[9] Sanrio consolidated its U.S. operations in California.[10]

It was Tsuji's decision to move into Asia in the 1990s that really put Sanrio on the map outside Japan. Asia now makes up 30% of Sanrio's overseas sales and still has potential for more. In Taiwan, Sanrio latched onto the "Japan freaks," these wannabes in Taipei who love Japanese cosmetics, pop music and sushi. Many have never been to Japan, though the number of Taiwanese visiting Japan has grown by about 50% between the mid-1990s and the end of the decade.[11]

Nowadays, packs of South Korea teenagers fill the streets of Tokyo's fashionable Ginza district hauling shopping bags full of Sanrio goods. Judging by the amount of their loot and the enthusiasm in their voices, shopping for Kitty is the highlight of their trip to Japan. Sanrio's Puroland, one-hour's train ride from central Tokyo, has also seen a bump in traffic from foreign tourists. About 10%, or 150,000, of its visitors come from abroad, especially Hong Kong and Taiwan. The company claims that since 1993, Puroland has had proportionately more foreign visitors than Tokyo Disneyland. "The prices are so high in Tokyo that Puroland is a relative bargain," said Kazuhiro Manabe, a public relations officer at the park.

The number of foreigners visiting the park really took off in 1996, Manabe said. This coincided with the rise in Asia's economies, but also the gradual weakening of the yen from its all-time high set in early 1995, making travel to Japan cheaper. The number of visitors from elsewhere in Asia, though, continued to rise even after the region was sucked into a financial crisis in the summer of 1997.

AN ASIAN AFFLICTION

There are many explanations for why Kitty took off in Asia, some of them cultural, some economic, some even political. One intellectual line of thinking has it that Asians are more attune to cartoon characters because many of the languages in the region use icons instead of alphabets. By processing information rich in graphics, Asians are more comfortable processing stories using pictures and symbols, most notably the Japanese *manga*. Certainly there is a long history of woodblock prints and other storytelling devices stretching back centuries, in Japan, China and elsewhere in the region.[12]

You don't have to look far to see that other countries in Asia also have their own culture of cartoons, particularly former colonies of Britain and France. The Japan Foundation Asia Center, for example, has held an Asian Cartoon Exhibition in Tokyo every year since 1995. The humor, satire and graphics at the exhibition in 2002 mirrored many of the sensibilities found in Japanese cartoons. Perhaps not surprisingly, Asian companies in South Korea, Taiwan and elsewhere – even seemingly sober operations like banks and steel makers – use cartoon characters as their mascots and in their logos, something that Western companies might shun for fear of looking childish.

Another theory posits that many Asian nations, having seen Japan grow into the region's first industrialized power, want to imitate and import Japanese culture. In other words, the "Japan as big brother" theory. There's a lot in this. In the 1970s, most of Asia was still years behind Japan in terms of economic development. But in the 1980s, Asia's Tiger economies were growing as fast as Japan did in the 1960s. In 1996, one year before its country's economy blew up, South Korea became the second Asian nation to join the Organization for Economic Cooperation and Development, or OECD, a kind of worldwide brotherhood of industrialised countries.

With the influx of foreign investment and strong receipts from exports, Taiwan, South Korea and other emerging economies in Asia developed larger middle classes that wanted to enjoy the fruits of their labor. That, in part, meant spending more of their excess income on luxury goods, travel, services and, it turns out, frivolities like Hello Kitty. By the early 1990s, Asia's roaring economies also included the next wave of young tigers in Thailand, Malaysia and Indonesia. While older generations of Asians were taught to shun Japanese cultural goods, younger Asians growing up in these countries knew little of the travesties of World War II. Instead, they saw Japan as a country that turns out hip karaoke, video games and *manga*. For them, buying into Japanese pop culture made sense.

In other Asian countries, like Indonesia, economic growth has given birth to a consumer class living modern, urban lifestyles that increasingly resemble those portrayed in Japanese *manga* and animation. Many prevalent themes, including children's empowerment and technological optimism, find rich soil in Asia's developing countries as well. Children in the region are generally better educated than their parents, and they are expected to lead the national march into a prosperous future. In such a setting, *manga*'s dream of a high-tech society built by the young generation finds strong resonance and support.[13]

Kitty's diplomacy helped overcome the fractious nature of Japanese-Asian relations. Historical animosities run deep in Asia, thanks to Japan's brutal domination of the continent in the 1930s and 1940s, when it turned many countries into colonies. Bad blood still flows. China and others routinely demand and receive foreign aid from the Japanese. Guilt money, some say. Into the late 1990s, South Korea banned "cultural imports" from Japan, preventing Japanese pop stars, artists and others from displaying their talents.

The cultural Cold War thawed in October 1998, when then-Prime Minister Keizo Obuchi went to South Korea and apologized for Japan's 35-year occupation of the country. In early 1999, South Korea lifted its two-decade old ban on imported Japanese consumer products. A year later, in June 2000, Seoul relaxed the ban on cultural imports, allowing South Koreans to import Japanese pop music, films and computer games.[14] In parallel, Sanrio's world ambassador for friendly relations, a.k.a. Kitty, was opening doors. By 2000, Sanrio had selected 20 licensees and opened 30 franchise shops in South Korea.[15]

This, of course, fed the frenzy for kids who do not remember the war. To them, Japan is held in high esteem. These younger Asians do not carry the emotional baggage of their parents and grandparents. In fact, many grew up watching translations of Japanese cartoons like *Astro Boy, Doraemon, and Sailor Moon*, the story of a high-school girl with super power, which is broadcast in nearly 20 countries. At its peak, the *Mighty Morphin Power Rangers* was aired in 80 countries.[16]

In effect, Japanese pop culture has driven a wedge between generations and united kids throughout Asia. "The young generation in Japan is more in touch with the young generation in Beijing and Bangkok than they are with their own older generations," said Frank Yu, an international branding expert who is also a rabid Hello Kitty collector. "To Asians, anything coming from Japanese culture is worth getting. The younger generations don't have the cultural hang-ups their parents did."[17]

Of course, Japanese companies aren't the only ones hawking their characters in Asia. Disney, Universal Studios and Warner Brothers also do a brisk trade. Disney's park in Japan is very profitable and the rest of Asia appears to be fertile ground for U.S. character companies. The government in Hong Kong was so desperate to have Disney open a theme park in the territory that it will pay about $2.8 billion to help build the park on Lantau Island. Disney will only put up about one-tenth as much, or $314 million, for a 43% share of the operation, which will open as early as 2005. Disney is also negotiating a deal to open another park in Shanghai, but it won't be first. A subsidiary of Vivendi Universal SA of France, Universal Parks & Resorts, expects to open a movie-based theme park in 2006.[18]

The popularity of these American brands does little to diminish Sanrio's hold on the Asian imagination. The Japanese company, after all, is homegrown. Ironically, Hello Kitty is technically British – she was born in London and the trappings around her are Western. The combination of her Asian design and Western storyline makes her unique.

Her popularity was certainly in evidence on the ninth floor of the Sogo department store in Hong Kong, where there was no shortage of choices for hungry fans. Wallace & Gromit, the British claymation figures, and Crayon Shinchan, a Japanese version of Dennis the Menace, were well represented in the character-goods corner. But the Hello Kitty section had the lion's share of the customers. In addition to small groups of schoolgirls, a half dozen women were dragging their kids through the aisles, which were stuffed with lunchboxes, towels and house slippers. The women without kids gravitated more toward the Hello Kitty handbags, wallets and bottled water. If you filtered out the Cantonese and English filling the air, you easily could have imagined you were in Tokyo.

Hello Kitty is also a hit with drivers, judging by the selection in the car-accessories section. There were pink stick-shift covers with Hello Kitty's face, Hello Kitty rear-view mirrors, glow-in-the-dark lighters for the dashboard and Kitty air fresheners. Essentially, everything a Kitty-crazed car fanatic would need.

Fans in Hong Kong have even taken to carrying pink Kitty credit cards, perfect for a power lunch. In 1998, Aeon Credit Card started distributing the cards, which were an instant hit. About 100 people a day lined up at the Aeon office in Central District, many of them men. By signing up for a card, applicants could choose a free Hello Kitty appliance.[19] (Hello Kitty was also at the center of a grisly murder in Hong Kong, which we detail elsewhere in the book.)

Kitty's resonance in Asia has far surpassed anything Sanrio imagined. In 2002, Hello Kitty was ranked the third most recognizable Asian brand, behind Sony Corp. and Cathay Pacific Airways, the Hong Kong carrier. According to the poll, Kitty is better known than Singapore Airlines, San Miguel and Singha beers, and Wipro, India's largest software provider.[20]

"HELLO KITTY, GOODBYE SANITY"

Kitty is much more than a brand. In some parts of Asia, she's an obsession. Hello Kitty has proven so popular in Singapore, Hong Kong and Taiwan that it has led normally docile people to riot. One of the best-known flash points was triggered by a joint campaign between Sanrio and McDonald's, the global fast-food chain. The frenzy started in Hong Kong in June 1999.

The companies joined hands by offering a stuffed Kitty doll with every "Happy Meal" customers bought. Sales boomed and McDonald's ran out of its entire stock of 4.5 million dolls in five weeks.

The cat-scratch fever spread to nearby Taiwan and on the first day of the campaign, McDonald's sold its entire ration of dolls – half a million – in just four hours, with Taiwanese braving long lines and intense summer heat to get their hands on the famous feline. The rage continued as the summer burned on, with each weekly stock selling out within hours of its launch. In all, 2.5 million of the dolls were sold in Taiwan, netting Sanrio a fixed commission and allowing McDonald's to earn $11.2 million in increased sales of burgers and fries. McDonald's "was smiling from the beginning to end in what they considered the best crowd-magnet campaign since the restaurant opened in Taiwan in the early '80s," said Benjamin Yeh, a spokesman at McDonald's Taiwan.[21]

The rush to get the dolls was more than just finding a collectible to keep your kid happy. The toys were actually a good deal. If you bought the doll separately, you would have paid NT$119, or about $3.50. But by spending between NT$99 and NT$129, you got not only a meal, but also the doll, that cost about half the price of buying it in a store.

Bargains were only part of the incentive. Customers in Hong Kong, Taiwan and Singapore saw an arbitrage opportunity, whereby they wanted as many of the limited edition dolls as they could find in case they could be resold for a profit. This was, after all, 1999, when eBay and other online auction sites were at their peak. Why not invest a few dollars now and perhaps double or triple your money tomorrow. "Asians love to horde things," said Yu, the branding expert who freely admits to owning a Hello Kitty video soccer game and a Hello Kitty doll-shaped clock that connects to your computer and talks in Japanese or English as you type on your keyboard (retail price: $89.99).[22]

It didn't take long for other companies in Taiwan to recognize the value of using Kitty to pitch their products. The Makoto Bank started plastering Kitty's moon-pie face on credit cards. The bank reportedly paid $295,000 to Sanrio as a licensing fee and spent another $3.5 million to market the promotion. The company quickly made its money back. In the first 10 months, about 400,000 customers rushed to the bank to switch cards. The new business generated $3.7 million in credit-card fees and the balance of revolving credit tripled, plus consumers plowed another $147 million into savings accounts to help pay for their credit card debts.[23]

Chunghwa Telecom Co. also got into the act when it unveiled a series of Hello Kitty phone cards. All 50,000 of the cards were gone in the first five minutes. Twinhead Computer followed suit, rolling out a notebook computer with Hello Kitty staring out from its pink cover. Yue-Loong Automobile even introduced a Hello Kitty car. To top it off, Kitty was voted the third most popular *person* in Taiwan, according to a Chinese Television Network poll.[24]

The rage spread to Singapore in January 2000. In another promotion, McDonald's offered a pair of Hello Kitty and boyfriend Dear Daniel dolls wearing wedding costumes from around the world to all customers who bought a Happy Meal. The problem was that an estimated 350,000 people lined up on the first steamy, rainy morning to get the dolls. Traffic jams formed outside McDonald's drive-ins as well.[25] Zealous fans cleaned out McDonald's supply in a few hours, with some customers buying half a dozen meals to get their prize and throwing the burgers in the trash.

Chaos broke out when the glass doors at the store in Block 22, Boon Keng Road shattered when too many people pushed against them. Shards of glass rained down on the queue and seven people were hurt. Three men were hospitalized. Singapore Civil Defense Forces were called in. To make things right, McDonald's employed security guards at its 113 outlets in the island-state. Earlier, two Singaporean men got into a brawl at a different McDonald's restaurant over Kitty dolls. To prevent further violence, the company figured out that a more sensible strategy would be to limit customers to four toys each. It might mean selling fewer burgers per customer, but would generate more foot traffic for the outlets and less bad publicity. The tactic worked. A year later, McDonald's launched another Hello Kitty promotion, this time with Kitty and Dear Daniel in costumes worn by royal families of India, China, Japan, England and elsewhere. This time, the cops were ready in Singapore and the promotion went off smoothly.

HAND WRINGING

The sales did more than keep kids happy, though. They exposed Hello Kitty to a lot of scrutiny and criticism, particularly by intellectuals and nationalists. It also triggered bouts of national soul-searching from Taiwan to Singapore. A year after the Kitty craze swept through Taiwan, intellectuals were still talking about how Kitty symbolized bald consumerism and how the Taiwanese have abandoned political and social movements. Critics even blamed Kitty for taking the steam out of the island's emerging feminist movement. Worse still, Kitty incited the not-so-buried nationalist fervor in Taiwan. It was bad enough going ga-ga for toys. It was worse to chase after *Japanese* toys, the nationalists said. It was yet another assault. The critics charged, "Hello Kitty is a Japanese cultural invasion, for it not only economically takes advantage of consumers, but also culturally degrades our popular culture," according to Yu-Fen Ko, a professor of communications at Hsih-Shin University in Taipei. "These critiques (sic) read the Hello Kitty fandom as symptoms of cultural Japanization, loss of feminist consciousness, or the fall of gender relations."[26]

But Ko argued that the nationalists and cultural elite have it wrong because they are out of date and unable to grasp that in modern culture, mass-produced characters are a way of life. He said Hello Kitty's popularity is another sign that life in Taiwan is in fact good, and that the people are now comfortable enough to indulge in a little frivolousness. "One claims that the popularity of Hello Kitty proves that Taiwan's democratization is successful because individuals are free to make decisions for his or her own happiness and no longer need to fight for human rights on the streets," he said.[27]

While Taiwan and South Korea continue to wrestle with their cultural identities, residents in Hong Kong and Singapore appear more comfortable with Japanese imports. Consumers in these two markets are smaller and depend on the outside world more. They also were both former British colonies, so have been exposed to Western consumerism longer.

China, too, is casting aside its wartime memories and embracing Japanese pop culture. As the country opens its doors to the outside, Japanese animation and video games are flooding in. In August 2002, 80,000 students in Shanghai flocked to an animation exhibit that featured 3,000 original drawings by Chinese cartoonists. The drawings, one Japanese cartoonist noted, were essentially rip-offs of Japanese drawings and this is a sign of their vitality. There are an estimated 80-million comic-book fans in China, where the animation market is expected to grow into a $125 million industry if publishing regulations are further loosened.[28] A growing familiarity with Japanese animation is bound to make it easier for Hello Kitty to take hold as well.

PACKAGING

Sanrio's success in Asia has no doubt been driven by Kitty's cuddly and seemingly universal appeal. But to get that message across, Sanrio, like many Japanese media companies, has learned how to package its products in a unique way. While some American media companies prefer to control as much of their distribution as possible, Japanese companies from different aspects of the media business routinely work together to publicize their products. This cuts into each company's share of the profits, but it also reduces costs because a television company does not need to become an expert at producing toys. These "image alliances" between publishing companies, bookstore chains, television broadcasters and merchandisers, which are common in Japan, and are now being formed to gain a foothold overseas.

The most extensive collaborations are in the music industry, which now encompasses not just recordings and concerts, but also videos and merchandising. "Many indigenous promoters and media organizations have collaborated with Japanese idol producers and promoters, facilitating a 'knowledge transfer' of Japanese-style idol production and marketing know-how to other Asian markets," said Hiroshi Aoyagi, an anthropologist at the Reischauer Institute of Japanese Studies at Harvard University.[29]

The practice has spread to other regions of the world and other types of products. Nintendo, for instance, rolled out its wildly popular Pokemon cards as its television series was filling the airwaves at home, and the timing was repeated overseas. Rival Konami took an even more deliberate approach. The company put together a consortium to publicize and distribute Yu-Gi-Oh, a character originally introduced in 1996 in the comic book, *Weekly Boys Jump*, that has sold more than 25 million copies in Japan. The multi-layered team of companies included Shueisha Inc., the publisher of the comics, Konami, which helped turn it into a video game, Upper Deck, the U.S. trading-card distributor, 4Kids Entertainment Inc., which put Yu-Gi-Oh on American television, among others. Sales of the cards in the U.S., for example, pulled in $17 million between April and June 2002, outpacing Pokemon.[30]

Sanrio's alliances have been less complex – like the promotional dolls at McDonald's – because its characters lack an ongoing storyline, so the company has invested less in television, video games and cards. Still, the company has broken ground by partnering Hello Kitty with other characters. One of the company's first experiments in co-branding came in August 2001 when Sanrio co-launched a line of limited edition accessories with Paul Frank Industries, maker of Julius the Monkey. The shoulder bags, purses, tee shirts and other items were sold through Paul Frank boutiques, Bloomingdale's, Nordstrom's and other department stores in the U.S. The character t–shirts went for $25 each.[31]

The collaboration came about by accident. In early 2001, Kitty's designer, Yuko Yamaguchi, was in San Francisco doing a promotional event at Gift Gate, the Sanrio retail outlet. During a break, Yamaguchi went shopping. Coincidentally, she ran into Paul Frank, who was signing his goods at a nearby shop. "I didn't know him well, but I had seen the monkey, Julius," said Yamaguchi. "So I went in to get his autograph. We exchanged business cards and I saw that on his card was a picture of him in his monkey pajamas, eating off a plate with a picture of Kitty on it!"[32]

When Yamaguchi returned to Tokyo, she and Frank, who lives in Los Angeles, started corresponding. Eventually, executives from Sanrio Inc. in the U.S. negotiated a deal with Frank. Yamaguchi went to Los Angeles to figure out how to co-produce Kitty and Julius. "It turns out that Frank is a goods planner, not a designer, so I ended up designing both characters and he designed the goods, which was a good division of labor," Yamaguchi said.[33]

That's the sanitized version of the story. Actually agreeing on designs to complement both characters and not subvert one or the other was not easy. In one mockup of the characters on a tennis court, Kitty hits an ace past Julius. In the final version, the ball is in the foreground and neither character has the upper hand. "They would say 'Kitty wouldn't do that.'

And I would say, 'Well, Julius wouldn't do that,'" Frank told *The Los Angeles Times*.[34]

The partnership was a reasonable success. The entire collection sold out, though there was no great rush at the stores.[35] The alliance also paved the way for another, more ambitious deal between Kitty and Tweety Bird, the wide-eyed canary owned by Warner Brothers. In November 2001, the two companies announced plans to have Kitty and Tweety together on about 200 products including stationery, fashion accessories and toys, which are sold throughout Asia. Notably, Warner Brothers will allow Sanrio to design exclusive Tweety products on its own to take advantage of Sanrio's expertise at marketing to women. "Both characters appeal to a similar audience – young women of today – and this partnership allows us to bring them together through creative, fashion-forward merchandise with a cross-cultural theme," said Mark Matheny, executive vice president of international licensing for Warner Bros. Consumer Products, when announcing the partnership.[36]

The deal came after about 10 months of brainstorming between Warner and Sanrio in the U.S. The idea to develop something "out of the context to promote both of our presence," happened quickly, said Bruce Giuliano, vice president of the licensing division at Sanrio Inc. in Los Angeles. "Then the legal departments took over," he said with a laugh. The deal was limited to Asia, though, because Sanrio is a less well-known brand in North America and the companies were "not sure that the American consumer would see the complementary nature of the characters," said Giuliano.[37]

KITTY'S STAR POWER

The companies do not release specific sales figures for these ventures. Nevertheless, the partnerships show not only how Sanrio has tried to cash in on Hello Kitty in the U.S., but also how visible – and desirable – she has become to American marketers. In fact, much to Sanrio's relief, globetrotting Kitty is riding a wave of popularity in the U.S., helping offset a dip in sales back home.

Similar to Sanrio's experience in Japan, Hello Kitty returned to stardom thanks to some unexpected help from nostalgic super models and singers. After going into hibernation for much of the 1980s and early 1990s, Hello Kitty started sprouting up when young pop stars like Mandy Moore, Christina Aguilera and Mariah Carey publicly pledged allegiance to the divine Miss Kitty. Tyra Banks took her Kitty handbag to the 2001 MTV Awards. Then Aguilera gushed, "I love Hello Kitty!" in *Seventeen* magazine. "I have this freaky doll that I travel with. When you press her paw, she sings the 'Hello Happy Song.' It's so cheezy, but it puts a smile on my face."[38] Aguilera, who also wore Hello Kitty jewelry on the cover of *Teen People* magazine, later went on the "Tonight Show" and annoced that she loved Hello Kitty gum.

"Christina Aguilera has done more for us than anything we could have paid her," said Giuliano. "She never gave an interview in a six-month period without mentioning Hello Kitty. You can't buy that kind of publicity."[39]

After years of slow growth in the U.S., Kitty is now popping up everywhere. Singer Mandy Moore took a Hello Kitty beaded bag to the Billboard Awards in Las Vegas in 2001, while pop diva Mariah Carey carried her Hello Kitty boom box to a record signing in New York. Singer Lisa Loeb couldn't stop herself either, hamming it up with Kitty in front of the new Sanrio shop in New York's Times Square. The shop, aside Disney on 42nd Street, is chock-a-block with Kitty favorites, including pink toasters for $34.95 (Kitty's face is imprinted on your bread), Kitty cordless telephones (made by General Electric) and Kitty dressed as the Statue of Liberty in, you guessed it, red, white and blue.

Loeb, one of the more outspoken Kitty fanatics among America's glitterati, can't seem to get enough of the stuff.

"Most of us work very hard and we're very, very busy, so anything that can add a spark of excitement and creativity and fun to mundane things in life is important to us," Loeb told *USA Today*.[40] Loeb even named one of her albums "Hello Lisa," and appears on the cover, with bow in hair, alongside Kitty wearing a pair of Loeb's signature glasses.

Sanrio also took part in the Girl's Rule Fall 2001 Fashion Show in New York's Bryant Park. Kitty has also become the toast of Fifth Avenue, where her button-nosed face is all the rage at Henri Bendel.[41]

"It's like an insiders' club," Tom Julian, of the ad agency Fallon Worldwide, told *Business Week* magazine, which ran a story on the rage for Sanrio's limited edition pink quilted bags that sold for $11.50.[42]

But Kitty is not just part of an insider's club for stars, she's a statement for those who want to snub their nose at the establishment. As detailed elsewhere in the book, Kitty has been adopted by some in the gay community. She's also made her way into boardrooms, where women executives have been known to flash Hello Kitty pens as a way to add whimsy and irony to corporate meetings. "We equate cuteness not with full citizenship," said Christine Yano, the University of Hawaii anthropologist. "As part of our individualism, Americans try to maintain a healthy distance from capitalism and from being manipulated." Showing off Kitty in normally sober settings affirms one's independence, even if it is tinged with humor, she said.[43]

Whatever the reason, thanks to Hello Kitty's rising visibility, Sanrio Inc.'s sales in North and South America have grown by a third since 1999 and doubled since 1995. The company raked in $96.32 million in the fiscal year that ended in March 2002, a figure the company expects to top in 2003.[44] Of the amount, about 55% is sold via wholesale outlets and 30% is sold directly to consumers at retail shops. The remaining 15% of Sanrio Inc.'s revenue comes from licensing fees.

The company has also moved south of the border. Sanrio opened a subsidiary in Brazil, Sanrio do Brasil Comercio e

Representacoes, Ltd., in 1987. It has expanded into Mexico, Venezuela and six other Latin American countries, where there are 89 Sanrio shops all together. Overall, though, the region has proven tougher to crack because of high tariffs on the importation of clothing and other goods. Sanrio is trying to set up alliances with licensees to outsource production within the region, a process that is taking time.[45]

However, the windfall of good publicity in the U.S. has turned into a different challenge. Giuliano said Sanrio has tried to "grow carefully" so as not to burn out the brand, something that has happened in other markets, he hinted. "We want Kitty to become very popular but not a fad. That's the challenge that we deal with."[46] But what can you do when Kitty is popping up everywhere?

Fortunately, pop stars aren't the only ones buying Kitty Sanrio now owns and operates 44 Gift Gate shops in the U.S. and licenses out another 77 Sanrio boutiques. Among them is the 1,900 square-foot marquee shop in Times Square and another major outlet in Honolulu's Ala Moana shopping center, a magnet for Japanese tourists on Oahu. Though these two shops are clearly targeted at tourists, most shops that sell Kitty and other Sanrio goods draw customers typical of the demographics in that area. Hispanics, for example, are big buyers of Hello Kitty in southern California. Sanrio also reckons that many of its newest customers in the U.S. are Asian, either tourists, or immigrants who continue to shop for Kitty in their adopted country. Kitty is also a popular item in Chinatowns across America.

She's also a hit online, though Sanrio is not pushing to become the next Amazon.com. Sanrio.com, the company's online sales channel for Kitty and other characters, attracts more than one million unique users a month. Hello Kitty was one of the top 10 most searched for toys on American Online's portal, too, in 2001.

The traffic is evidence of how quickly Kitty's visibility in America has grown. In a survey conducted in May 2002, Sanrio found that 83% of the 18-to-34-year olds polled recognized Kitty, while the brand awareness among kids between six and eleven years old was 72%. Though Americans do not give gifts as often as the Japanese, Sanrio has focused on these girls (and they are almost all girls), as well as young women between 18 and 25 (who make up about 35% of sales), two groups that "are really into sharing," as Giuliano explained. "Although there are substantial differences between the U.S. and Japan, within that age group, they are the same."[47] Like in Japan, young mothers in the U.S. are starting to deck out their children in Kitty newborn and infant apparel and accessories.

Kitty has taken off, as in other parts of the world, in parallel to the interest in Japanese animated character goods. The company's market research shows that Americans uniformly think Kitty is cute. Instead of trying to reinforce this message, which seems to be getting across with little effort, Sanrio focuses on what products might hit it off with shoppers. Through word of mouth and clever packaging, the appeal of the Kitty brand has grown quickly. So quickly, in fact, that many people do not even realize Kitty was created in Japan. "It doesn't matter to most people where she came from because they are drawn to the character itself, not necessarily where she originated from," said Laura Takaragawa, a licensing marketing manager at Sanrio Inc.[48]

Kitty's brand – and kitsch – appeal has been reaffirmed on eBay.com. Random searches net 8,000 or more Kitty items on the world's largest online auction site. Idle shoppers could have snapped up a Hello Kitty Louis Vuitton Pink Flower Bag for as little as $39, or even a Ladies Hello Kitty G-String Thong for those sexy cats. There are even some enterprising souls in Hong Kong still trying to flog their limited edition stuffed dolls, in their original plastic wrappers, for $15, the same ones they picked up with their Happy Meals at McDonald's in 1999. Sanrio doesn't seem perturbed that fans are making an extra buck off of Kitty as long as they are not knock-offs. The company believes it reinforces the Sanrio brand rather than weakens it. Besides, it would be hard to stop the selling.

CONQUERING THE OLD COUNTRY

After working decades to crack the American market, the company is also making strides in Europe, which makes up another 10% of Sanrio's overseas sales. Kitty made her first paw print on the continent in 1980, when Sanrio set up a branch office in Hamburg, Germany, an outfit that became a subsidiary called Sanrio G.m.b.H. three years later. Kitty got a lukewarm reception in Europe even though she is technically a British citizen, having been "born" in London in 1974.

But Japanese animation now has a small but steady following among children in Britain, France, Germany and Italy, where Pokemon, Konami's Yu-Gi-Oh and other television cartoons have caught on. These shows, the growing number of Toys 'R' Us shopping outlets and Sony's hit PlayStation 2 game console have helped popularize American and Japanese toys in Europe. British adults, who have an eye for the absurd, have caught the Kitty bug. There's even a Sanrio shop on Oxford Street in London to prove it. Like in the U.S., Kitty also has star power. Former Spice Girl Gerri Halliwell is a big fan, having been spotted toting luggage emblazoned with Kitty's face. Other, more ordinary, women in their 20s and 30s who want to add a dash of whimsy to their lives have been smitten with Kitty. "Hello Kitty is my passion and my life," gushed Maidi Smith, a 32-year old woman from south London who started collecting Kitty in 1998. "I must have spent thousands of pounds since I started collecting her. She's like a drug but, instead of being a bad thing, Hello Kitty is pure and innocent, there is nothing nasty about her."[49]

KITTY, THE CROSS CULTURAL CAT

Whether it's London, New York or Singapore, Sanrio often wrestles with how to package Kitty in ways that will make people shell out their hard earned cash. Doing this is not as easy as sticking Kitty's face on products. Some things, it turns out, are lost in translation or, worse, amplified in the wrong ways when they cross the Pacific. The simple explanation for this is that Sanrio's designers do not understand American sensibilities as well as the American marketers on the ground in Los Angeles or San Francisco.

The export and import division in Sanrio's headquarters routinely works with designers in the U.S. and elsewhere to come up with new products. The ideas go the other way too, since American designers sometimes have a better sense of what colors are "in" that season, a particularly important issue since Kitty is often sold as a fashion accessory.

There is also a different emphasis in the two countries. While Sanrio has more than 80% of Japan's "fancy-goods market" – essentially, high-end products with characters on them – the company has only a 1% share of the U.S. market,[50] even after a quarter-century in America. Some products, like expensive handbags, might sell well with Japanese consumers but appear too costly for Americans, who prefer t-shirts and other low-cost items. "There is criticism from the Japanese side about [our] cheapening the market, for example by entering the apparel business," said Etsuo Iida, executive vice president at Sanrio Inc. in Los Angeles. "We try to select certain designs, but the Japanese designers say that the color and pose selection are not good for this age group."[51]

Choosing products, though, isn't the only problem, Iida said. Sometimes, the content of the product does not translate across cultures. For example, one Sanrio design included Dakko-chan, a plastic black doll, and a penguin eating watermelon, items that would have raised alarm bells with U.S. civil rights groups concerned about racist symbols . "Even though it's okay in Japan to print 'Even I can count 1-2-3' on a card that has a picture of a black boy, it looks as if you are saying he has a low IQ to an American," Iida said. "The Japanese don't have any sense of guilt or sin. It always feels like there's a language barrier and cultural differences in the decision-making process. The people I interface with in Japan come from their own experience and they try to implement their Asian model in the U.S." Because of run-ins like these, Sanrio has more or less given up trying to customize Kitty for each market, and now tends to make one design to fit all cultures, with small adjustments along the way. In the 1990s, the company put Kitty in the local clothes and surroundings of Taiwan and Hong Kong. The move failed because, as the company discovered, Asians buy Kitty *because* she is Japanese, or at least from Japan. In other words, her unique Japanese packaging – cute beyond belief, a hint of Western influence combined with a dash of Japanese culture, like a kimono – is what sets her apart from Mickey, Snoopy and the blizzard of other characters.

One exception to this is the localized Kitty goods that have proven to be a big hit in Japan. Sanrio Inc. in the U.S. has launched two lines of Kitty products set in Hawaiian and New York motifs. She poses with pineapples in Honolulu, for example, or as the Statue of Liberty at some shops in New York. "It's a concept that enhances her collectability via a new sales channel," said Bill Hensley, Sanrio Inc.'s marketing director. The company is also considering releasing Kitty in a Western motif (Cowgirl Kitty?), as a Las Vegas showgirl and as a Florida beach bum.[52]

HEADING FAR EAST

Sanrio's import-export department isn't the only part of the company focused on markets overseas. Sanrio Far East Co. (SFE), a wholly owned subsidiary, takes care of two other crucial functions. First, the company and its staff of about 40 are one of Sanrio's main links to its production facilities in China, where about half of all the company's goods are made. Second, SFE runs a licensing business that represents other companies' characters and brands in Japan.

The company is largely the brainchild of Yasushi "Andy" Toyama, who joined Sanrio in 1976 just as Kitty was taking off. He spent eight years in America, including five years in New York in the early 1980s, when Sanrio had an office in the city's Fashion District on 7th Avenue. (In the 1980s, Sanrio moved briefly to Rockefeller Center. Sanrio left New York entirely a few years later, and now has a representative office in Fort Lee, New Jersey.) When Toyama returned to Tokyo in 1985, he went to work in the import-export division to put his knowledge of overseas markets to use.

As it turned out, 1985 was also the year the Group of Seven industrialized nations agreed to deliberately weaken the dollar and strengthen the yen and other major currencies. The goal was to reverse America's chronic trade deficit with Japan, which was being accused of dumping its goods in the U.S. The result of this agreement was that the yen doubled in strength to about ¥120 between 1985 and 1989.

The dramatic reversal made Japanese products more expensive for those buying them with dollars, the currency of choice in international trade. Toyama's customers overseas started complaining that they could no longer afford to import Hello Kitty and other Sanrio products, which were made in Japan and priced in yen.

So Toyama, with Tsuji's blessing, looked for places to produce Sanrio goods offshore, particularly textiles. He went first to Taiwan and South Korea, Japan's two closest neighbors, but the best manufacturers already had their hands full with other Japanese clients. So Toyama went to Hong Kong, which had modern shipping and banking facilities and was the gateway to China. Most Chinese manufacturers, though, preferred U.S. customers who placed larger orders than the Japanese. Eventually, Toyama convinced a handful of Chinese manufacturers that Sanrio was interested in a long-term deal that would include some small, but also some large, orders.

With Toyama in charge, the factories made goods for Sanrio's licensees who sold them overseas. "Selling these Chinese goods was okay for the overseas market," he said, "but Sanrio felt it wouldn't look good if people saw 'Made in China' on goods sold in Japan." There were problems at the outset, but instead of switching suppliers because of their shoddy work, Sanrio worked with these companies to refine their operations. The quality steadily improved. "We didn't fool around with a lot of different manufacturers," Toyama said.[53]

As the quality improved, the folks in the head office got over their snobbery and realized how much money they could save. To keep the lines of communication clear, Sanrio Ltd., the parent company, set up its own subsidiary in Hong Kong that would essentially mimic Toyama's work. But instead of supplying Sanrio's licensees, the Hong Kong office would supply the parent company, which then sold the goods directly to consumers.

Eager to use its connections in China, SFE started representing other companies that wanted to produce there. SFE is a production agent in Asia for the cosmetics giant, Avon, and it helped Disney produce kids' suspenders in China, too. In all, SFE helps supply 120 companies, including Sega and Philip Morris.

LICENSING AGENT

As China has modernized, finding a partner in the Middle Kingdom has become less of a mystery and fewer companies need Sanrio Far East's expertise. So Toyama started representing other companies' brands in Japan. SFE has landed big accounts, including Coca-Cola and Campbell's Soup. SFE helps produce and market Coke's line of tee shirts, glasses and other collectibles that the company sells via a website and a specialty shop in Tokyo.

Toyama has said that SFE wanted to triple sales generated by non-Sanrio characters to about ¥6 billion ($50 million) by 2003[54], a figure that has proven too optimistic. In fact, SFE's total sales (including its outsourcing businesses in China) were only ¥5.8 billion ($48.3 million) in fiscal year 2002, and the licensing of other companies' characters make up only 10% of that total.[55]

Still, the company is gaining ground. It helped design, produce and distribute all the goods sold in Japan for the FIFA World Cup in 2002. The company now represents more than two-dozen companies and expects to double that figure in 2003. According to Toyama, the strategy is not to target kids' characters that compete with Sanrio's lineup, but to concentrate on older brands that have long histories. "When we say licensing in Japan, people usually think of characters," Toyama said. "At this moment, these have peaked and no one has a crystal ball to predict when they will become popular again. But because of their history, Campbell's, Coke and others, will be around for another 30 to 50 years."[56]

ENDNOTES

[1] Carmel Li, personal interview via e-mail, Oct. 2002.

[2] Douglas McGray, "Japan's Gross National Cool," *Foreign Policy*, May-June 2002.

[3] Ibid.

[4] Sanrio Inc. and Warner Bros. Consumer Products, Nov. 15, 2001, "I 'Tawt I 'Taw A Hello Kitty Cat."

[5] Nadine Willems, "Japan Goes to Asia," *Winds Magazine*, Aug. 5, 2001.

[6] "Hello Kitty Goes Worldwide," *Nikkei Weekly*, Dec. 18, 2000.

[7] "Sanrio to Open First Shop in China," *Nihon Keizai Shimbun*, Oct 9, 2002.

[8] Christine Yano, Associate Professor, Anthropology, University of Hawaii, personal interview, Feb. 4, 2003.

[9] "Kitty Hopes Americans Will Say Hello," *The Japan Economic Journal*, Apr. 14, 1990.

[10] Bill Hensley, marketing manager, Sanrio Inc., personal interview, Feb. 8, 2003.

[11] Willems, 5.

[12] For a good introduction to the history of graphic storytelling, see Frederick Schodt, *Manga! Manga! The World of Japanese Comics*, Kodansha International, 1983.

[13] Saya Shiraishi, *Doraemon Goes Abroad*, quoted in Craig, 302.

[14] Mark Castellano, "South Korea Eases Ban of Japanese Culture," JEI, No. 26, July 7, 2000.

[15] Kunio Endo, "South Koreans say hello to Kitty, other Japanese cultural exports," *Nikkei Weekly*, July 24, 2000.

[16] Andrew Pollack, "Japan: A New Superpower Among Superheroes," *The New York Times*, Sept. 17, 1995, Business section.

[17] Frank Yu, international branding expert, personal interview, Jan. 13, 2003. Yu now works for Microsoft Corp. in Singapore promoting the company's X-Box video game console.

[18] Lara Wozniak, "Crouching Tiger," *Far Eastern Economic Review*, Jan. 23, 2003, 24-26.

[19] Cesar Bacani and Murakami Mutsuko, "Pretty in Pink Slump," *Asiaweek*, Mar. 19, 1999.

[20] http://www.brandingasia.com/survey/survey.htm.

[21] Benjamin Yeh, McDonald's Taiwan spokesman. Quoted in Susan Fang, "Hello Kitty: Taiwan's billion dollar fad," http://test.ieatpe.org.tw/tit/tit2_16.htm.

[22] http://www.dreamkitty.com/Merchant2/merchant.mv?Screen= PROD&Store_Code=DK2000&Product_Code=K-FB109141&Category_Code=HK.

[23] Susan Fang, "Hello Kitty: Taiwan's billion dollar fad," http://test.ieatpe.org.tw/tit/tit2_16.htm.

[24] Yu-Fen Ko, assistant professor, Dept. of Public Communication Hsih-Shin University, Taipei, "Hello Kitty and The Identity Politics in Taiwan," Oct. 2000. Speech found at http://www.isop.ucla.edu/circa/paper/tw_ko.pdf.

[25] Chong Chee Kin, "Hello Kitty, Good-Bye Sanity," *Straits Times*, Jan. 14, 2000, http://bundleoflove4.tripod.com/theunofficialhellokittywebsite/id21.html.

[26] Ko, 15.

[27] Ibid., 8.

[28] Toru Kono, "Comics and Animation Hot with Young Chinese," *Kyodo News*, Oct. 3, 2002.

[29] Hiroshi Aoyagi, "Pop Idols and the Asian Identity," Craig, 318-319.

[30] Ken Belson, "Rival to Pokemon Keeps Market Hot," *The New York Times*, Oct. 6, 2002, Sunday Business Section.

[31] "Sanrio to Launch Kitty, Julius Monkey Joint Goods in U.S.," Jiji Press, June 29, 2001.

[32] Yuko Yamaguchi, personal interview, Sept. 10, 2002.

[33] Ibid.

[34] Hilary E. MacGregor, "Well, *Hello* Kitty: Julius the Monkey Meets His Match," *The Los Angeles Times*, Aug. 20, 2001.

[35] Bill Hensley, marketing manager, Sanrio Inc., personal interview, Feb. 8, 2003.

[36] Sanrio Inc. and Warner Bros. Consumer Products, Nov. 15, 2001, "I 'Tawt I 'Taw A Hello Kitty Cat." Mark Metheny in press release, Nov. 15, 2001.

[37] Bruce Giuliano, personal interview, July 26, 2002.

[38] Heidi Sherman, "Life in the Fast Line" *Seventeen*, July 2000, p. 120.

[39] Giuliano, personal interview, July 26, 2002.

[40] Kelly Carter, "Hello Kitty is the Cat's Meow," *USA Today*, Apr. 22, 2002, Entertainment section.

[41] Jill Gerston, "Feeding the Kitty," *The Los Angeles Times*, Dec. 27, 2002, Calendar section.

[42] Julia Cosgrove, "Cat on a Hot Thin Model," *Business Week*, Sept. 10, 2001, Up Front section.

[43] Yano, personal interview, Feb. 4, 2003.

[44] Katsumi Murakami, CFO Sanrio, Inc., personal interview via e-mail, Feb. 8, 2003.

[45] Bill Hensley, personal interview, Feb. 8, 2003.

[46] Giuliano, personal interview, July 26, 2002.

[47] Ibid.

[48] Laura Takaragawa, licensing marketing manager, Sanrio Inc., personal interview, July 26, 2002.

[49] Isla Whitcroft, "Hello Kitty – the ultimate in kitsch," *Now*, May 23, 2001, 50-51.

[50] Giuliano, personal interview, July 26, 2002.

[51] Etsuo Iida, executive vice president, Sanrio Inc., personal interview, July 26, 2002.

[52] Bill Hensley, marketing director, Sanrio Inc., personal interview, Feb. 8, 2003.

[53] Yasushi "Andy" Toyama, personal interview, Jan. 28, 2003.

[54] Yumiko Ono, "Sanrio Plans to Expand Product Design Business," Dow Jones Newswires, May 18, 2000.

[55] Toyama, personal interview, Jan. 28, 2003.

[56] Ibid.

Chapter 5

Kitty Kulture

As office buildings go, the headquarters of the Federation of Japanese Banks is about as somber as you can get. Facing the outer moat of the Imperial Palace in central Tokyo, the glass and stone building is as unremarkable as it is unfriendly. The drab 1970s faux-modern exterior, the dusty, stone-cold lobby and the forlorn rent-a-cops at the front door ensure that this place will never be mistaken for a nightclub.

But as you sign in at the reception desk, a careful glance to the right will reveal one of those curiosities that only seem to make sense in Japan. There, about five feet high, is an antediluvian glass showcase. It's the lonely, forgotten type of display you'd expect to see stuffed with meaningless awards and plaques that never get dusted. Look closer though, and you'll find a collection of foot-sized dolls: a naked baby named *Kewpie*, the powerful action hero, *Ultraman*, and even *Winnie the Pooh*. The three-dozen or so characters are the mascots of Japan's largest banks.

That a bank normally considered the bedrock of the business community, the sober and silent place where you entrust your life savings might have a mascot is not entirely surprising. Banks, like all businesses, have to market themselves and develop corporate personas. They also need to add a dash of humanity to otherwise steely and impersonal images.

But most banks, at least in the West, prefer to emphasize their rock-solid reputations to reassure their clients big businesses, salarymen and their wives. Many use conical shapes, stiff right angles and thick brush strokes to convey their image. Adopting doe-eyed cartoon characters to help shape their corporate identity would be like Citibank choosing the Pillsbury Dough Boy as its mascot. By falling over themselves to find the cutest character to represent them, Japanese banks seem to be targeting school kids and infantile adults who need to be told that banking can be fun. Or are they?

In fact, these banks are doing what many companies in Japan do: Using graphic images, particularly cute ones, as displays and logos. They are so common in Japan that to be without one is odd. Unlike in the U.S. and Europe, cartoons, animation and comics are not reserved just for children, but are woven into the fabric of nearly every public and private space. Visit any city center and you'll see signs, flyers, walls and other common ground covered with the stuff. Cartoon characters fill living rooms, desks and even the windshields of dump trucks.

Manga are also everywhere in Japan and targeted at every imaginable demographic group. Central and local governments, the police force and even the Self Defense Forces use cartoons in their advertising and pamphlets. Every year the oh-so-sober Ministry of Finance prints a booklet called "Let's Talk about Taxes." On the cover is a three-generation family of chirpy cartoon characters who appears throughout the document besides tables illustrating tax rates and income brackets. Electric utilities and construction companies, not to mention schools, sports teams and Olympic squads also use cartoon characters. Japan's biggest advertising firm, Dentsu, developed a new-employee handbook in the form of a *manga* and hired Kenshi Hirokane, author of the famous comic strip, "Division Chief Kosaku Shima," to write it.

There are cartoons for kids, of course, including Hello Kitty. But young boys, teenagers, girls, college kids, businessmen and housewives can all find comics that cater to their tastes and dreams. Educators have also found it easier to get kids to read their history books if they are graphically enhanced. Animated movies, too, are a huge industry. Some of the biggest grossing films are animated, as evidenced by Hayao Miyazaki's *Spirited Away*, a cross-generational hit that won the Oscar for Best Animated Feature in 2002 and has been shown at about 800 theaters in the U.S. In short, Japan is a wonderland of graphic arts.

The fascination with all things graphic stretches back decades and even centuries, depending on how you define it. This suggests that though Hello Kitty is a unique character in modern-day terms, she has grown out of a long heritage and has been incorporated into a culture that is thoroughly comfortable with and comforted by storytelling and the graphic arts. "Japan is a country that is traditionally more pictocentric than the cultures of the West, as is exemplified in its use of characters or ideograms, and *anime* and *manga* fit easily into a contemporary culture of the visual," according to Susan Napier, who has written extensively on animation.[1]

As we discuss elsewhere in the book, Hello Kitty has no particular storyline, so strictly speaking is not part of the tradition of *manga* and animated television and video cartoons. But she is at the center of the culture of cute, or *kawaii*, that is one of the more recent and successful efforts to commercialize the graphic arts. While Americans are addicted to fast-talking action heroes, Hello Kitty proves that graphics can be the core attraction for many Japanese fans. "Such a great amount of graphic content is produced in Japan that you don't need a story" to go along with the character, said Marcia Aoki, a licensing executive with a major U.S. company in Japan.

"The graphics are the story. There's a deep appreciation of words not spoken. It's ingrained in the culture."[2]

Hello Kitty and cute culture, though, are only one of the most recent permutations in the history of storytelling through pictures. The rich variety of graphic arts in Japan helps explain why Kitty and characters like her are so easily accepted in everyday life in Japan. This high comfort level with characters and pictures has turned the country into a fertile breeding ground for Sanrio and others to experiment with new products and designs. While Sanrio in the U.S. spends money on marketing studies to figure out what consumers want, in Japan, the company just scans key neighborhoods in Tokyo. It's as if the society is one big focus group to experiment with characters.

This broad acceptance of the graphic arts has been turned into a multibillion-dollar industry and taken center stage in the global licensing market. Japanese companies like Sanrio, Bandai, Nintendo and Konami have drawn on this rich tradition and packaged and distributed it to hungry audiences overseas. We'll discuss these companies that have become world leaders in churning out characters. But first, let's take a look at their roots.

WAY BACK WHEN

The origins of *manga* are richly debated in academic circles, and though this section is not meant to provide an exhaustive explanation of the history of graphic arts, *manga* and other related topics, there are certain themes that are worth mentioning. There are some, for instance, who claim comics and cartoons are so much a part of Japan's culture that they go back a millenium or more, to the seventh century, when characters and caricatures adorned newly built temples. Other academics trace today's pop culture back to the 12th century and the legendary Bishop Toba, who wrote the *Animal Scrolls*, a humorous narrative that turned animals into talking creatures to poke fun at the clergy of the day.[3] These and other drawings were the province of the landed and literary classes, so rarely seen by the masses.

It wasn't until the Edo Era, which lasted from 1603 until the shogunate collapsed in 1868, that the graphic arts were brought into the mainstream and commercialized.[4] During the long rule of the shogun, an urban, bourgeois culture expanded as money and power concentrated in Edo, the ancient name for Tokyo, and a handful of other cities. As mercantilists grew fat serving the shogun and his network of courtiers, they had money to gain access to some of the same pleasures previously reserved for nobles. During this time, novels and drama, particularly *kabuki* theater, evolved.

The real vehicle for distributing cartoons, though, was woodblock prints, the production of which was mechanized in the 17th century. Most woodblock prints were single frame comics, but some were also assembled into whole pamphlets. Though the shogun's totalitarian regime censored much of this work, artists found ways not just to convey beauty, but also political and sexual satire. *Ukiyo-e*, the art of the "floating world," grew into its own unique art form that would later inspire Impressionist painters in 19th century France. "Like so much of old Japanese art, *ukiyo-e* projected a spare reality: without dwelling on anatomy and perspective, they tried to capture a mood, an essence, and an impression — something also vital to caricature and cartooning," according to Frederick Schodt, author of *Manga! Manga! The World of Japanese Comics* and one of the leading scholars of Japanese animation.[5]

Artists also utilized a ready-made selection of animist characters from Japanese folklore and myth like the *kappa* (a goblin-like cross between a monkey and a turtle), *kitsune* (fox) and *tanuki* (a raccoon-dog), characters that were later turned into trademarks. "The monsters weren't hard to work with because there was such a great supply of them, and their entertainment value has not decreased," said Adam Kabat, a professor of comparative culture at Musashi University in Tokyo, and author of several books on mythical monsters.[6]

Combined with new innovations in printing technology and a wider audience for the material in Japan's growing cities, the graphic arts were democratized, popularized and commercialized. Woodblock prints, often with erotic images from the Yoshiwara red-light district of Edo, became souvenirs for visitors from outside the capital. Cartoons poking fun at politicians of the day were also big sellers, even though artists risked arrest from wary culture cops, but these artists couldn't resist making a quick buck.[7] There were even early precursors of what later would become Pikachu and Doraemon. "More than 200 years ago, Edo culture was already reinventing traditional folklore to produce its own consumer-oriented monster boom," said Kabat.[8]

The collapse of the shogunate in the second half of the 19th century and the opening of Japan's borders to the outside world unleashed a whole new set of creative impulses. Almost overnight, the Japanese began importing all things Western as the country's businesses and government embraced what they thought were the best aspects of American, British, German and French life. One import, perhaps unintended by the aristocrats bent on catching up with the West, was comic books, which were then popular with boys in the U.S., Britain and elsewhere. The Japanese were great admirers of several British and American cartoonists who plied their trade in Yokohama, where foreigners were forced to live in the latter half of the 19th century. The imported illustrated stories blended easily with Japan's own traditional narratives, creating a new medium that, by and large, remains today.

In the same way, the Japanese also imported techniques used in Western marketing and advertising and regurgitated them to fit Japanese tastes. At the Advertising Museum of Tokyo, visitors can see many early 20th century Japanese advertisements, which look much like ones found in London, Vienna and Paris. Advertisements for Hero cigarettes, for instance, featured a Western sailor while posters for the Hoshi drug company included a blond angel sitting on a sun with *Fin de Siecle* calligraphy along the borders. Many other ads also incorporated Edo-era cartoon figures and illustrations.

Characters were not just limited to single advertisements; they became stand-alone logos. Tofu Kozo, or Tofu Boy, was one such Edo-era character that made a comeback in the 19th century as a kind of patron saint of sweets shops. Statues of the stumpy boy carrying a tray of tofu sat outside stores to attract customers. Unlike other mythical characters, though, Tofu Boy didn't do much of anything and little in the way of a story was attached to him, very similar to that button-nosed feline who has taken the world by storm. "Tofu Boy is a true 'character monster' in that with his trademark tray of tofu, he is instantly recognizable even though he doesn't do anything per se or have any story — an Edo version of Hello Kitty," said Kabat.[9]

POST-WAR BLOSSOMING

Like in other parts of the world, the 1920s was a tumultuous decade in Japan when the Taisho democratic reforms came into full, if brief, bloom. Cartoons during the period became politicized, particularly by those associated with the Communist Party. While British and French cartoons were influential before the turn of the century, American-style comics held sway after World War I. American newspapers were filled with "funny pages," another concept the Japanese imported, along with the idea that comics could be tailored for kids.

The Japanese also turned comic strips into books, which ran color illustrations and allowed writers to develop longer storylines. Bound as volumes, they became permanent parts of family libraries. Japanese comic artists took a physical form imported from the West, combined it with a centuries-old Japanese tradition of narrative art and illustrated humor, and added important innovations of their own to create what amounted to a totally new genre.[10]

As Japan tilted towards war in the 1930s, the cartoon industry came under pressure to conform to the mores of the military government. During World War II, many artists were drafted into writing propaganda or uplifting, if unrealistic, stories to mollify the masses. Some even produced leaflets and other disinformation that were dropped on enemy troops. The few writers who refused to participate were jailed.

After the war, the American Occupation maintained some controls on the industry, but as freedom of speech gradually returned, the *manga* industry blossomed. In the days before television, *manga* was one of the few cheap forms of entertainment available. In the immediate post-war period, the industry was centered largely in Osaka, where small start-up publishers printed cheap "red book" comics, so called because they used red ink. But as writers and publishers grew in influence and wealth, they moved to Tokyo.

It was during this period that Osamu Tezuka (1928-1989), the man widely considered the father of the modern *manga*, came into prominence. A former medical student, Tezuka incorporated Western film techniques into his comics, which were largely devoted to kids. "I experimented with close-ups and different angles," he wrote in his autobiography, "and instead of using only one frame for an action scene or the climax (as was customary), I made a point of depicting a movement or facial expression with many frames, even many pages."[11]

To accommodate Tezuka's more expansive style, *manga* grew longer and larger to display the illustrations more effectively. The folksy nature of his comics influenced a whole generation of writers to become cartoonists. Unlike movies, the theater and other art forms, the cost of entering the *manga* industry was far lower. Tezuka's influence grew along with the industry as his hits like *Tetsuwan Atomu* (*Mighty Atom*) and *Shintakara-jima* (*The New Treasure Island*) triggered rapid growth of the industry. In all, Tezuka penned more than 150,000 pages of *manga*.

More than a dozen years after his death, Tezuka's influence survives, as does the Japanese affection for *manga*. Tezuka's most famous character, Mighty Atom, better known as Astro Boy, was given honorary residency status by Niiza City north of Tokyo on April 7, 2003, Astro Boy's 50th birthday. Niiza is home of the studio where Tezuka produced the popular feature. The town's mayor, Kenji Suda, pushed for the honor, which the current president of Tezuka Productions, Takayuki Matsutani, happily accepted. "We would love for our city to take after the Mighty Atom, energized by his 100,000-horse powers," Suda said. Never mind that foreign residents have trouble establishing residency; *manga* characters are larger than life.[12]

One of the turning points in the development of the industry came in 1959, when Kodansha, one of Japan's largest publishing houses, issued a weekly, instead of monthly, *manga*, a step other publishers quickly followed. Now, writers had to pump out four times as much material and the extra work required for more writers to take up the craft. The public loved the growing selection and sales boomed. *Manga*, books and magazines were quickly available in bookstores, at train station kiosks and in vending machines. They are read in barbershops, on trains, in coffee shops and at home — places where they serve as handy sources of entertainment.[13] The *manga* industry has grown to about $5 billion a year and *manga* now make up about 20% of all magazines and books sold by value, and 40% based on the number of copies.

A large part of *manga*'s appeal is its cost. For just a dollar or two, readers can flip through an easy-to-read thriller that strings you along from week to week. The magazines are perfect for killing time on long train rides to the office. "The popularity of *manga* has been linked to poverty, and long and dull commutes between home and work place," wrote Sharon Kinsella in *Adult Manga: Culture and Power in*

Contemporary Japanese Society. "Adult and boys' *manga* has been a portable television set for men who work long hours. For 40 years, *manga* provided the cheapest and most easily available form of entertainment in post-war Japanese cities."[14]

During the 1960s, *manga* turned into vehicles for political activists and experimentalists. Students also became active readers, particularly those who wanted to rebel against their parents. Reading *manga* instead of weighty college textbooks was the literary equivalent of turning on and tuning out. The government, backed by housewives' and teachers' associations, cracked down on what it considered subversive material, pressuring publishers to tone some of it down.

Publishers saw that politically combative comics hurt the industry's image and threatened their business, so a measure of self-censorship followed. A handful of larger publishers emerged through mergers and bankruptcies, giving them more power over writers and artists. To counter claims that *manga* led to slothfulness and produced political and social deviants, publishers launched a campaign to show that *manga* was part of Japan's long cultural history and therefore worth preserving. "The opposition to *manga* and animation industries by conservative elements in post-war society has encouraged the defenders of *manga*, namely professional *manga* critics, to emphasize or even invent stylistic origins for *manga* in ancient Japanese history," said Kinsella. "Its critics have hoped that if they could prove that *manga* is, somehow, a part of *traditional* Japan, then it cannot possibly be uprooted and repressed by the government."[15]

As the corporations that ran the industry grew larger, they took *manga* mainstream in the 1970s and 1980s. They developed more magazines for various segments of the population, particularly for young boys and girls. The introduction of "*shojo*" *manga*, as girls' cartoons are called, was one new genre actively targeted as a consumer group. Women authors were recruited to develop *shojo manga* comedies, dreamy fairytales and other themes. The *shojo* comics set the stage for *kawaii* culture, the promotion of consumption seemingly for its own sake and, ultimately, Hello Kitty and other characters.

Shojo is all about consumption, consumption as pleasure, as play, and as a creative act. The *shojo* is pure, innocent, delicate, cute, romantic and ephemeral, like girlhood itself, explained Julianne Komori Dvorak, a graduate student at the University of California ar Berkeley. "Like the prewar *shojo* magazines, Sanrio was marketing an aesthetic. If the old *shojo shumi* was characterized by sweetness, sentimentality and dreaminess, the new *shojo shumi* that came into its own during the fancy-goods boom of the 1970s and 1980s was characterized by cuteness," she said.[16]

As *manga* grew more sophisticated, the formerly rebellious baby boomers turned into parents. Having grown up reading *manga*, they weren't about to deny their kids the same pleasure. So much to the consternation of teachers and grandparents, kids raised in the 1970s and 1980s were allowed to indulge freely in their favorite comics and television shows. This fueled demand for even more shows. "Parents aren't so strict with young kids these days," said Hiroshi "Hank" Nozaki, a special advisor to the Tokyo Foundation, which sponsors an academic course devoted to *manga* at Waseda University in Tokyo. "Parents are so strict with young kids [about other things] so they allow them to spend a few hours a day with *manga*. And kids have no reason to stop reading *manga* when they get older. Someone can be a social success and still read *manga*."[17]

Though *manga* are still widely read throughout Japan, sales have slowed as the economy has weakened. Baby boomers, the main consumers of *manga* during the first few postwar decades, are now starting to retire and are reading fewer comics. Young Japanese, too, are flocking to video games, *anime* on television and using the Internet more. In years past, school kids on long commutes to school would read *manga* to pass the time. Now, many play video games on Nintendo's GameBoy and send messages to their friends via their cell phones.

While sales have stagnated at home, a surge of interest in *manga* has come from overseas. Japanese animated cartoons are staples on U.S. and European television and kids in the West are looking for the original cartoons that inspired the shows. *Shonen Jump,* one of the most popular Japanese weekly comics, is printed in English and attracted 10,000 subscribers even before it was released in November 2002.[18] The same month, Gutsoon! Entertainment, Inc. in the U.S. launched Raijin Comics, a weekly *manga* based on Japanese stories and characters that are translated into English. Gutsoon! Entertainment expects to sell about 15,000 copies per week, targeting readers between 15 and 34 years old.

College campuses have also become breeding grounds for *manga,* transcending the long-held stereotype in America that comics are only for young kids. The University of California at Los Angeles and three other schools in the state system will begin teaching a course in *manga* and *anime* in 2003, the first of their kind in the U.S The course, "*Manga & Anime*: Expressions of Japanese Culture and Society," will be taught by Japanese instructors and funded by the Tokyo Foundation.

MANGA GOES VIDEO

As Japan grew prosperous in the 1950s and 1960s, television became a central part of everyday life on the archipelago. The Japanese are among the most avid watchers of the boob tube in the world, and one big reason for this is *anime*. The sheer variety of these programs is mind-boggling: From the upbeat and family-oriented *Sazae-san* series to the hyper kinetic "*Dragon Ball Z.*" Many of these programs are derivative of *manga* and follow after the print version by several months or years, depending on the production requirements. *Anime* television shows have also morphed into movies, videos and DVDs. About half of all films now released in Japan are *anime*.

The popularity of television around the world has helped disseminate *anime* much faster than *manga*. School kids in the U.S., Europe and most recently China, are now fed a steady diet of Japanese *anime*, including at various points Sailor Moon, the Mighty Morphin Power Rangers and the now-ubiquitous Pokemon. Japanese television studios produce about 50 series a year and about as many for videos, a growing portion of which are converted for export. Companies like Disney are now forming ventures to distribute *anime* in the U.S. The word *anime* has become so well known that it made its way into a *New York Times* crossword puzzle.[19] In all, about 75 *anime* television shows and movies were released in America in 2001, a tenfold increase compared to a decade before.[20] The market for *anime* videocassettes and DVDs in the U.S. should hit $500 million in 2003.[21]

To meet American sensibilities, many *anime* are refashioned before they are exported. Nudity and extreme violence are cut. Some *anime* also whitewash references that can be construed as offensive to religious viewers, like the inclusion of witches and dark forces. Some references that only Japanese can understand have also been altered.

Though Japanese *anime* and *manga* producers try to conform to local mores, they feel more comfortable letting it be known where the content originated. For older generations in the West raised on Speed Racer and Godzilla flicks, Japan meant camp. But to younger kids today, Japanese shows featuring Pokemon, Yu-Gi-Oh and One Piece mean quality and innovation.[22]

Americans, like the Japanese, are drawn to *anime* because the storylines are generally more complex than many American cartoons, which often rely on slapstick and fights between good and evil. Japanese *anime* wrestle with a wider range of themes including gender conflict, romance, horror and comedy. More often, too, stories carry from one episode to the next, keeping kids glued to the set. Movie versions of the television show, the "crossover" market, catch additional viewers. There is also less cynicism and fewer inside jokes that only adults can understand. Instead, the show speaks more directly to kids. There is a rather sharp contrast with current American pop culture, with its heavy doses of cynicism, "attitude" and putting people down.[23]

Manga's more unifying messages and uniqueness in America bond viewers. Conventions are held across the U.S. that attract a wide array of fans, from young kids to students of Japanese to adults. Many show up dressed as their favorite characters, a kind of permanent Halloween party where fans can swap videos and watch new releases. "A lot of this isn't necessarily about *anime*," said Mike Tatsugawa, who runs the Society for the Promotion of Japanese Animation in the U.S. "It's about a community."[24]

GAMES GALORE

Perhaps the most lucrative offshoot of Japan's graphic tradition is video games. Sometimes lumped together with toys, video games, both the software and hardware, are in fact an industry unto themselves. According to the International Council of Toy Industries, the industry was worth almost $15 billion worldwide in 2000, and though still one quarter the size of the toy industry, it is one of the fastest growing segments. It's also the battlefield of global giants like Sony, Microsoft and Nintendo, which compete by selling consoles; and a slew of other companies, like Konami, Sega and Electronic Arts, which provide the software.

The sales of consoles and software generate far broader economic benefits than just printing comic books and airing television shows. The consoles, require high-powered semiconductors and other equipment that create jobs for workers in many industries unrelated to character goods. The sales of the consoles and software are also symbiotic, driving demand for one another. "There is a link between hardware and software sales in that both feed off each other," according to Mina Sawamura, an analyst at the rating service, Moody's Japan. "New software titles encourage demand for new hardware, while higher hardware shipments lead to the launch of new games."[25]

Some companies are able to combine software and hardware under one umbrella, most notably Sony and Nintendo, which produce more than half the software for the GameCube console. The Kyoto-based Nintendo hit it big with the release of its Pokemon video game, which accounted for more than one quarter of the company's sales in 1999. The company parlayed that success into hit movies and a television show, generating more than $1 billion in sales of licensed goods and other merchandise in Japan.[26] The company has also shown an amazing knack for reviving the characters after sales started to wane. In 2002, Nintendo released a new Pokemon television show that was tied more closely to the game software it released. The *Monthly Korokoro*, a leading *manga*, also ran a new serialized Pokemon cartoon to reinforce the message, a total package that Nintendo has learned to assemble as well as any of its rivals.

"The multimedia equation in Japan, with the *Monthly Korokoro* comic at the kernel and comics, toys, animation and games all working toward a common goal, is well established, and it is very common for game makers and toy makers, too, to use a multimedia approach that uses the *Monthly Korokoro* comic to gain exposure when launching new contents," said Soichiro Fukuda, an analyst at Nikko Salomon Smith Barney, a Tokyo brokerage house.[27]

While some games are created with entirely new characters and plots, there are no shortages of existing titles in Japan to work with. Konami, for instance, turned its Yu-Gi-Oh card game, which itself was an offshoot of the original comic, into a video game. Since there are 2,000 cards in the game, Konami has plenty of material to use when spinning out new versions. Even the demure Miss Kitty hit the screens in a 2002

World Cup soccer game that can be played on home computers. The three-dimensional game allows users to play a "Friendly Match," a "Tournament" or against friends in a "Multiplayer Match" via a local area network.

In 2002, the top-selling video game in Japan was Nintendo's "Pocket Monster – Ruby Sapphire," which sold 3.19 million units, three times more than the next best seller.[28] Despite this success, Japan's videogame makers earn the bulk of their profits overseas. Japan's game software market contracted more than 30% to $3.1 billion[29] between 1997 and 2001 as the economy slogged through two recessions. At the same time, the game software market in the U.S. surpassed $10 billion for the first time in 2002, growing 9.6% from a year earlier.[30] The number of game consoles grew by 10%, though price cuts by Sony and other makers pushed down sales in dollars by 4%.

The 60% decline in console prices, however, turned previously pricey items into mass-market toys, helping boost software sales. Video game sales in the U.S. jumped 21% in 2002, driven by games like Grand Theft Auto: Vice City, Madden NFL 2003 and Super Mario Sunshine. Another game, Spider-Man: The Movie, also did well as its release coincided with the popular film of the same name. This kind of multimedia release will become increasingly popular in the years ahead. "There is a barrage of new game software launches that will appeal widely to new video gamers, both old and young, expanding the software-to-hardware tie ratios of the previous generation," said Richard Ow, a senior account executive at The NPD Group, which tracks the gaming industry.[31]

Nintendo, Sony and Konami, in particular, are very skillful at packaging these media products because they have better access to original graphic content like *manga*. With close contacts with publishers in Japan, they can adapt *manga* for television or video games, and wait for the *manga* writers to develop storylines that lend themselves to being packaged in another medium. "In Japan, that's the business model from the beginning," said Nozaki, from the Tokyo Foundation.

"When writers develop cartoons, they are already thinking of the media mix."[32]

Worried about Japan's slumping economy and relying too heavily on the American market, Japanese game makers are now eyeing Europe. Video software maker, Capcom Co., is moving to Germany to distribute its software titles faster and, it hopes, boost its European sales from the current 20% to 30% of company-wide revenue. Another software writer, Koei Co., aims to triple its European sales to $42 million in three years. Though both companies operate subsidiaries in London, where they can distribute software already developed in English for the U.S. market, they are finding additional buyers in Germany, France and Italy.

Having seen the success of these increasingly global software companies, the Japanese government is trying to promote the industry at home by making it easier for venture companies that produce movies, games and animation to raise funds. The Ministry of Economy, Trade and Industry, which estimates that Japan's digital contents industry grew 13% to $15.8 billion in 2002,[33] has set up a study group to find ways to remove regulations that prevent content providers from acquiring capital. The measures are designed to solve a constant problem in Japan: How to get money to start-ups. Policymakers know that banks have an easier time grasping how manufacturers do business than a software venture with a fuzzy business model. Many bankers, too, were burned during the Internet bubble when software-related investments fizzled.

That lawmakers are finally grasping the potential of these contents industries, shows how far Japan has come in the more-than-40 years since Tsuji set up Sanrio. Back then, the government poured all its resources into building a manufacturing super power, funneling the country's vast savings into banks that in turn provided cheap capital for makers of steel, electronics and cars. Many of these industries can now stand on their own. Many, too, have moved offshore to compete with neighboring China, Korea and Singapore.

The government needs new businesses to drive the economy and contents industries show vast potential.

TOY STORY

Ironically, back when Tsuji started Sanrio, Japan was derided in the West as a country only capable of making cheap toys, which were then one of the country's best-known exports. "Made in Japan" was stamped on model airplanes, toy soldiers and plastic knick-knacks. Now, Japan seems to have come full circle. Not only is it the second largest retail market for toys, worth $13.3 billion in 2000,[34] but companies like Bandai, Takara and Tomy have become world leaders in the industry.

So far, few companies have produced a toy with the staying power of a Barbie. Instead, the majority of toys that have gone global have turned into fads, like Takara's Bowlingual toy, which "translates" a dog's bark in Japanese and other languages. It has sold well enough in Japan that the company started exporting it in 2003. The hit is reminiscent of Tamagotchi, the digital chick released by Bandai in 1997. The company went on to sell 20 million of the egg-shaped toy, but it went rotten a few years later, just like the Pet Rock and other fads. Indeed, many Japanese toys targeted at fickle school kids turn out to be one-hit wonders, an occupational hazard all companies grapple with, Sanrio included. "If something gets too big too quickly, it implodes," said David Buckley, president of Copyrights Japan, an agency that coordinates programs for licensors of characters or brands. "You need to keep the public enthused, without letting it grow too quickly."[35]

That's why toy makers including Sanrio are always looking for new audiences. In recent years, they have turned their attention to people in their 20s and 30s who want to recapture some of their youth by buying limited-edition Barbie dolls, G.I. Joe action figures and reprints of rare Superman comic books. By one estimate, adults buy 35% to 40% of the action figures sold in the U.S.[36] "We adults want to get back to history, to their own history and to their childhood, the days when they felt very happy," said Thomas Kohnen, product manager at Idee+spiel, an association of German toy retailers.[37]

Still, the market selling toys to the working set is not big enough to offset the decline in the number of children. This demographic time bomb is something all entertainment companies wrestle with, particularly in Japan, where the declines are more noticeable. This explains why Japanese content providers, like manufacturers in the decades before them, are using Japan as a kind of hothouse for growing characters and then unleashing them overseas where profits can be higher. Given its hyper-competitive, yet richly textured market, if a character succeeds in Japan, it stands a decent chance in other countries as well. "In the international consciousness Japan remained a serious nation and people, accomplished in traditional arts and modern manufacturing, but hardly a wellspring of entertainment and appealing cultural creations that would one day spread beyond Japan's shores," wrote Timothy Craig in *Japan Pop!: Inside the World of Japanese Popular Culture.* "Today it's a different story. Japan's pop culture has not only continued to evolve and blossom at home, it has also attracted a broad, street-level following overseas, giving Japan a new cultural impact on the world to complement its established economic impact."[38]

ENDNOTES

[1] Susan J. Napier, *Anime: From Akira to Princess Mononoke: Experiencing Contemporary Japanese Animation* (New York: Palgrave Macmillan, 2001), 7.

[2] Marcia Aoki, licensing executive with more than two decades experience in Japan and the U.S., personal interview, Feb. 20, 2003.

[3] Frederick Schodt, *Manga! Manga! The World of Japanese Comics* (Tokyo: Kodansha International, 1983), 28.

[4] Craig, 7.

[5] Schodt, 34.

[6] Adam Kabat, professor of comparative culture, Musashi University, personal interview, Aug. 3, 2002.

[7] Ibid.

[8] Adam Kabat, "Monsters as Edo Merchandise," *Japan Quarterly*, (2001): 66-77.

[9] Ibid., 75.

[10] Craig, 8.

[11] Osamu Tezuka's autobiography, as quoted in Frederick Schodt, "*Manga, Manga!*," Kodansha International, 1983, 63.

[12] Kyodo News, Mar. 19, 2003, translated by Arudou Debito.

[13] Mark Wheeler MacWilliams, "Japanese Comics and Religion," in *Japan Pop!*, 110.

[14] Sharon Kinsella, *Adult Manga: Culture and Power in Contemporary Japanese Society* (Honolulu: University of Hawai'i Press, 2000), 200.

[15] Ibid., 19-20.

[16] Julianne Komori Dvorak, "*Sailor Moon* and the Shojo-ization of Male Imagery" (Unpublished M.A. thesis, University of California, Berkeley, 1997), 3-13.

[17] Hiroshi "Hank" Nozaki, special advisor, The Tokyo Foundation, personal interview, Feb. 27, 2003.

[18] Kim Curtis, "U.S. Publisher Latches Onto *Manga* Mania," The Associated Press, Nov. 26, 2002.

[19] Napier, 7-13.

[20] Jesse McKinley, "*Anime* Fans Gather, Loudly and Proudly Obsessed," *The New York Times*, Sept. 3, 2002, Arts Section, 1.

[21] Tokyopop, a Japanese comic book seller, as quoted in the *Nihon Keizai Shimbun*, Mar. 25, 2003.

[22] Debbi Gardiner, "*Anime* in America," Japan Inc., Jan. 2003.

[23] Craig, 13.

[24] McKinley, *The New York Times*, Sept. 3, 2002.

[25] Moody's Ratings Outlook for Japan's software industry, Jan. 30, 2003.

[26] Sian Rees, "What a Character!," American Chamber of Commerce Journal, Jan. 2001, 44-47.

[27] Soichiro Fukuda, Nikko Salomon Smith Barney report, Jan. 8, 2003.

[28] Ibid.

[29] *Nihon Keizai Shimbun*, Jan. 27, 2003.

[30] The NPD Group, Jan. 27, 2003.

[31] Ibid., http://www.npd.com/press/releases/press_030128a.htm.

[32] Nozaki, personal interview, Feb. 27, 2003.

[33] "Content Developers Finding It Easier To Procure Funds," *Nihon Keizai Shimbun*, Jan. 13, 2003.

[34] International Council of Toy Industries.

[35] Rees, 46.

[36] Miki Tanikawa, "Adults want to play, too," *The International Herald Tribune*, Oct. 12-13, 2002, 13.

[37] Ibid.

[38] Craig, 4.

Chapter 6

Defiling Hello Kitty

It's an ugly, heartless and extremely violent world out there. And while Hello Kitty embodies all that is sweet and precious to some, then there are the unbelievers, the blasphemers, the anti-cuties, that cross-section of humanity that gets a kick out of making fun of Hello Kitty, defiling her or otherwise exploiting her in an untoward way. Internet pornographers have expropriated Hello Kitty's image to promote their sites. In Japan, the vast adult entertainment industry, the so-called pink trade, have played the same game as the moon-faced character's image is splashed on advertisements across the windows of public telephone booths much to the consternation of Sanrio's legal team. Who wants Hello Kitty soliciting for massage parlors and "dating clubs" in Tokyo? Social satirists have had a field day poking fun at a Sanrio they believe cranks out a lot of cheap sentimentality. The vast toy-making workshop that China has become is a particularly lethal threat to Sanrio's franchise. All manner of knockoff goods are streaming out of Chinese ports and clearing customs across Asia and Europe. Sanrio figures it loses as much as $800 million or so a year in sales to such counterfeiters.

Asian-American feminists think Hello Kitty is emblematic of an entire range of values — largely submissive ones — that feed into male chauvinism throughout Asia and foster a misguided, simplistic and patronizing form of Orientalism among white males in the U.S. Some even argue that this has spawned a huge demand of Asia bridal-search sites on the Internet. Others just loathe the cat simply as a matter a taste. Its syrupy message triggers a gag reflex in many souls. And education-obsessed mothers, the type that send their kids to Montessori schools and ban Barbie and PlayStation 2 from their kids' reach, think Hello Kitty is a dangerous strain of commercially inspired brainwashing. It equates design with happiness. That, in turn, misleads young minds about the way the world really works, so the thinking goes. Life is more of a contact sport and less of a tea party with cookies and apple pie. And by slapping Hello Kitty on every product under the sun, the indictment continues, this cartoon character is the ultimate commercial whore, a signifier of unbridled and soulless consumerism.

So let's just stipulate right here and right now, that a lot of people out there have Hello Kitty issues. This roiling parallel universe of Hello Kitty haters is sometimes just a nuisance. But others can and have done the brand some commercial harm. Small wonder Sanrio has a full-time legal team of about a dozen lawyers tending to some 400 outstanding lawsuits as of the end of 2002. It also sends out on average about 50 warning letters a month to those it alleges are infringing on Hello Kitty's copyright in some manner. Sanrio's legal eagles can, and often do, identify and dissuade defilers of Hello Kitty. But this cat belongs to a vast, seething and multifaceted global culture. And sometimes she gets caught up in some very bizarre situations that Sanrio can't do very much about. Though Sanrio has been fending off rip-off artists and cranks for decades now, nothing quite prepared them for the likes of Chan Man-lok, Leung Shing-cho and Leung Wai-lun, the convicted perpetrators of what came to be known internationally as the Hello Kitty murder. How could they? In early 1999, this trio of unemployed men with ties to the Triad, or Hong Kong's criminal gang, held Fan Man-yee, a 23-year-old bar hostess, captive in their flat for roughly a month, tortured her brutally and later dismembered her corpse and stuffed her skull into a Hello Kitty doll.

KITTY HOUSE OF HORRORS

The sheer brutality of the case and the Hello Kitty angle were a no-brainer storyline for the international media, which pounced in the usual ravenous way. When the most lurid details came out during the trial, headlines such as *"Severed Head Hidden in Hello Kitty Doll"*[1] and *"Hello Kitty Murder Case Horrifies Hong Kong"*[2] started ricocheting around the global media echo chamber. The basic facts of the case add up to the following: First, the three took Fan hostage after a dispute about money. She was then beaten daily, sometimes with metal pipes or strung up by her hands with electrical wire. After she died, they dismembered her body with a saw, boiled her internal organs and (for reasons probably best left unexplored) developed a cameo role in this horrific case for Hello Kitty. That turned out to be a colossal blunder, however, for these sick puppies. For eventually a 13-year-old girlfriend of one of the killers, contacted police after being wracked with guilt.

When police finally checked out her story and visited the flat in Hong Kong's Tsim Sha Tsui district, they walked into one of the most stomach-wrenching scenes imaginable. According to an account in the *South China Morning Post*, detectives found Fan's "badly decomposed heart, lungs, liver and intestines in a bag on the canopy" of the building.[3] Fan's skull and lower jaw had been sewn into a Hello Kitty doll. Detectives found a human tooth next to Kitty. As Hong Kong prosecutor Mike Arthur would later tell a jury hearing this case, but for the sheer stupidity of the Triad members and the lucky break of a guilt-ridded witness, Fan's captors might well have gotten off scot-free. "These three men nearly got away with murder. Had they not left the skull, tooth and internal organs, there would have been no trace of Fan Man-yee. All that would have been left was the nightmares of a teenage girl," he intoned.[4]

After weeks of excruciatingly nauseating trial coverage, Sanrio officials probably thought they would get some respite from the bad Hello Kitty publicity once the trio were convicted and sent off to prison to finish out their days. Instead, their angst levels shot up into an entirely different realm when they found out that a local filmmaker decided to do a dramatic treatment of the case under the working title: *There's A Secret in My Soup*. Great, the Hello Kitty murder was about to become a cult film in Asia, and possibly, beyond. Sanrio sent off a flurry of letters and warnings that Hello Kitty absolutely not appear in the film in any capacity at all. Publicly, the Japanese toy maker condemned the filmmakers for exploiting a grotesque outrage and by extension sullying the Sanrio ethic of "love, friendship and happiness." In the end, the filmmakers backed off and agreed not to include Hello Kitty's role in the grisly tale.

THE WILD, WILD WEB

Happily, these kinds of public relations challenges — skulls being stitched into your franchise products — are quite rare. Yet to a certain type of mind and imagination there is a bit of malicious pleasure that comes with teasing Hello Kitty, toying with her, ripping out her whiskers and using her to promote, say, a sex club in Tokyo. Sometimes, these scoundrels and detractors are just hitching a ride on the cat's iconic status around the globe. But more times than not, these types just have a real problem with Kitty and the values she represents.

The cute vs. anti-cute cultural wars are currently raging all over the Internet. Hello Kitty, it seems, just gets under some people's skin.

This comes in all forms and modes of expression, sometimes a little on the sophomoric side. How much do I loathe thee, little Kitty? One website called Kitty Poems counts the ways with malicious little ditties that mercilessly shred Sanrio's central message that a happy, cute face and little precious things can somehow bring us a little closer together.[5] Against a backdrop of Sanrio characters, this site showcases some poems as this:

> *Porno Kitty*
> *Come, Kitty Kitty, come, kitty kitty*
> *I will pay you lots of money*
> *If you will just participate in my Porno Flick*
> *Come, Kitty Kitty, Come, Kitty Kitty*
> *I will make you a really big star*
> *She is a porno kitty*
> *MY Porno Kitty*
> *Come, Kitty Kitty, come, Kitty Kitty*
> *I see you have lots of talent*
> *Let me be your agent*
> *All you have to do is sleep with me*
> *And I will get you the role of a life time*
> *Oh it's right here in my very own porno flick*
> *She is a porno kitty*
> *MY Porno Kitty*
> *Are you a slut kitty*
> *or a whore kitty*
> *or a porn star kitty*
> *Or are you just a little Horny Kitty*
> *What are you?*

Google your way around the web in search of Hello Kitty links, and it isn't hard to find some pretty bizarre takes on the deeper meaning of a cartoon character. Though Sanrio's product design team probably didn't give much thought to the fact that Hello Kitty has no mouth, plenty of detractors are clearly miffed. Sometimes they strike out against Sanrio with scathing satire. One website came up with an extensive list of reasons for the missing orifice. Our favorites include:

- Hello Kitty has no mouth, but she must scream. That is why her head is so big.
- Hello Kitty wept for she had no mouth, until she met a man who had no face.
- Hello Kitty has no mouth, and yet in space you can hear her scream.
- Hello Kitty has no mouth, and yet children are starving in Africa.
- Hello Kitty has no mouth but hey, cocaine goes up your nose.[6]

Well, you get the idea. Hello Kitty also gets ripped in a question-and-answer format by the imaginative (demented?) minds behind another site, whose creators are referred to mysteriously as the two Tims. Here is one of the more amusing ones:

Question: Why does Hello Kitty have no mouth? Plus, why does everyone think you are dissing Hello Kitty? You are just telling the truth. I have been a fan of Hello Kitty for many years, but have always wondered what the Sanrio company is trying to keep Hello Kitty from saying. I think that all she wants to say is that we are all special in our own way. Is the Sanrio company part of a conspiracy to keep hate and prejudice alive? Hello Kitty is beautiful!

Answer: Why does Hello Kitty have no mouth? This is truly the crux of the problem. Unfortunately, only Sanrio and Hello Kitty herself know the answer, and Sanrio isn't talking either. A number of theories have been advanced:

First, and most common, the Sanrio Conspiracy. There is something which Hello Kitty knows and which Sanrio doesn't want out. She was therefore deprived of her mouth, and kept constantly in the public spotlight so that she would have no opportunity to do anything about it. A variant on this theory is that the fame is Sanrio's way of buying her off.

Secondly, the Unfortunate Mutation theory. Hello Kitty was once a normal kitten, but then something happened... something horrible... and so she was mutated into a creature with a huge head and no mouth. This is supported by the fact that Spiderman, who was turned into a super-powered mutant by a radioactive spider bite, has no visible mouth either. The nature of the accident which could have caused this is shrouded in mystery and uncertainty.

Thirdly, the Unwitting Pawn theory. This is very similar to the first theory in that it casts Sanrio as a ruthless de-mouther of cats. In this theory, Hello Kitty has no special secrets to be protected, but Sanrio is merely using her to satisfy its sadistic needs for power and silence.

We still do not know for sure which of these theories, if any, are the truth. All we know for sure is that Hello Kitty has no mouth.[7]

HELLO KITTY AS PERFORMANCE ART

Hello Kitty has also been batted around the performance art community. In late 2002, the visual and performance art theorist Jaime Scholnick held an exhibit at the Post Gallery in Los Angeles called, *Hello Kitty Gets a Mouth*. Passersby at the gallery were entertained by a hilarious 10-minute video that is broadcast on a Hello Kitty television in a recreated and extremely precious bedroom. Juxtaposed against that sweet scene are nearby-wall-sized images of Hello Kitty-like figures in violent settings. The storyline kicks off with Hello Kitty getting ready for bed. She slips off her Hello Kitty slippers, and nestles herself between her Hello Kitty sheets and then reaches for her Hello Kitty vibrator. But in Scholnick's rendering, Hello Kitty can't express pleasure, for the simple reason that she has no mouth. She then hurls the vibrator across the room in a hissy fit and thus begins Hello Kitty's private odyssey to get a mouth. In Japan, she is turned down by one plastic surgeon after another and ends up traveling to the nip-and-tuck capital of the Western world, Beverly Hills.

Other images interspersed in the plotline add up to a highly ironic commentary on why the kind of overwrought cuteness that Hello Kitty embodies isn't all that it seems. Schnolick, who received a master of fine arts from Claremont Graduate University, lived in Yamagata, Japan during the early 1990s. She went there to explore contemporary Japanese art and teach English. She left somewhat appalled by the second-class citizenry of Japanese women and how the country's "cute" ethos encourage women to play submissive roles. When even her middle-aged students starting showing up with Hello Kitty gear — pins, pens, handbags and so on — Schnolick channeled her anger into a one women-show at a gallery in Tokyo called "*Kawaii/Kowaii*," a play on the Japanese words signifying cute and scary. It was a multimedia work that included cat dolls in cages and with blackened eyes. That same kind of dramatic tension was clearly on display in *Hello Kitty Gets a Mouth*, at least in the opinion of one reviewer:

> The sense of outrage that simmers beneath the demure humor of the video — outrage that grew specifically out of Scholnick's experiences living in Japan but which isn't limited to the scope of that culture alone — bubbles to the surface in several wall-sized chalk murals depicting Hello Kitty figures in ski masks waving machines guns. Spare in comparison — the roughly 4-foot characters float against flat fields of black and hot pink. Impeccably rendered, these murals are both playful and vicious.

The guns appear to spew only thin ribbons of color, yet the walls are scatter with violent black marks resembling bullet holes, suggesting that power often comes in deceptive package.[8]

Another example of the kind of searing intellectual criticism that rightly or wrongly is directed at the "cute" value system that Hello Kitty represents, comes from Asian-American feminists such as Denise Uyehara who runs Fearless Hair Theater Productions out of Santa Monica, California. One of the solo performance pieces she has done is called *"Hello (Sex) Kitty — Mad Asian Bitch on Wheels."* Go to her website and you'll see Uyehara holding a gun to Hello Kitty's head. Her show is described in the following manner:

A heartfelt and humorous exploration into love, dating and sexuality, this work excites all genders to laugh, talk and respect each other. Uyehara tells it like it is through the Vegetable Girl, the Mad Kabuki Woman, an Asian dyke and an Asian guy. She tackles "that Asian male/ female thang" in "The Joy Fucked Up Club," examines love, violence and respect among men and women, discusses HIV/AIDS, and gives the real deal on women loving women.[9]

And if you are wondering about the reviews, there are also some blurbs full of critical praise, for *Hello (Sex) Kitty* provided on the site. The *Labyrinth Philadelphia Women's Newspaper* pointed out that Uyehara, "describes making love as an opportunity to see, if only for a moment, a person with the layers stripped away ... we are naked at the moment of orgasm, and it is then that our true selves are visible through the eyes." Like Scholnick, Uyehara subverts and distorts the image of Hello Kitty to score rhetorical points about feminism and gay culture that it's safe to say would make the character's caretakers at Sanrio cough up fur balls. This piece, according to Uyehara, "is a parody response to Hello Kitty and to the cute ideas I grew up with. Hello Kitty was always an icon I never had, but the really cool girls had."[10] During this performance, which Uyehara has performed in Los Angeles, London and Beijing, she bounces back and forth between two alter egos. One is a Hello Kitty-inspired character called Vegetable Girl. She likes cute things and pines for a white boyfriend who admires all things Asian. The other is the Mad Kabuki Woman, which is the complete antithesis of everything sweet and precious, and likes to tell men "to go and suck their white patronizing dicks." Uyehara ends the show by stripping herself naked and standing silently in front of a mirror for three minutes.

ANGRY ASIAN GIRLS

Interestingly enough, it seems the budding Asian-American feminists' movement on the West Coast just can't resist turning Hello Kitty into a voodoo doll to promote their ideologies — and, in some cases, pull a Sanrio by turning out t-shirts, trinkets and stickers that promote anti-cute images. Consider the website called "Big Bad Chinese Mama" created by Kristina Wong.[11] It is a pretty hilarious send-up of your typical online mail-order website that promises to set up Western men with nubile Asian women, nodding violets, meek and gentle souls who are less abrasive and confrontational than American and European women, or so goes the common stereotype. The display page features a defiant Hello Kitty, with a mouth and a speech bubble that says: "I am ready for ya asswipe." The site also features Kitty stickers that promote the website's URL address and Hello Kitty spouting obscenities such as, "Get this fucking bow off my head."

Like Uyehara, Wong wants to take a wrecking ball to stereotypical images omnipresent in Western mass media. In Wong's world, or at least her website, such brokered Asian brides are loud, vulgar and angry women, who don't tolerate fools gladly. Instead of sexy photos, focused on cleavage and biographies that stress youth and purported Asian values of deference toward men, Wong's online brides are shrews that like to kick white men in the shins and otherwise bruise and insult. In her satirical frequently-asked-question section, one can find this exchange:

> Question: I am a generous Caucasian man looking for a loyal, soft-spoken, and dainty Asian woman (sorta like the exotic Suzy Wong in *The World of Suzy Wong*). Can you assure me that you will find me such a demure creature on your site?
>
> Answer: What the fuck? Are you so preoccupied with your patriarchal colonialist longings of global conquest and cultural commodification that you think those kinds of mythical people exist? Reality Check. The women that are featured on real mail-order bride websites are Third World women who come from poor families and social status who are forced to enter the multibillion dollar sex industry by working in "sex resorts" or being sold off as mail-order brides. The women in real mail-order bride websites do not "fantazize" about loving you, but seek overseas marriage to escape the usually brutal and semi-slave-like conditions that living as a sex worker entails.[12]

Hello Kitty hasn't gone unnoticed in the broader gay community, either. In the early 1990s, a well-known gay journalist, designer and bon vivant in the Los Angeles art community developed the equivalent of the Antichrist Kitty that made quite a splash. Jim Yousling, who had once edited a gay skin magazine called *In Touch For Men*, developed a character called Hell Kitty, which started showing up on t-shirts all over the country and drove the folks at Sanrio into a state of high dudgeon. Yousling, who died of an AIDS-related form of cancer in 1995, was remembered by one obituary writer in the *LA Weekly*, for his clever rework of Hello Kitty.[13]

Jim's master stroke was Hell Kitty, a demonic, disobedient spoof of the irrationally saccharine and over-marketed cartoon character ("Hello Kitty Loves You"), complete with pitchfork, piercings and cute, winking asshole. Hell Kitty committed acts of arson, diddling and sacrilege a full 10 years before MTV's boorish toons, and with a lot more style. Naturally, it met with foul play at the hands of Sanrio, Hello Kitty's humorless corporate owner.

On the flip side, Sanrio has tried to promote a more positive image of its Hello Kitty brand by teaming up with such groups as YouthAIDS, a group working in some 60 countries to promote "decreased sexual activity, protected safer sex and abstinence," according to the YouthAIDS website. Such companies as Levi's, which has issued a jacket for the campaign, and the Magic Johnson Foundation have lent their support. Sanrio for its part, allowed the group to develop a special t-shirt, to further the group's educational aims. It features Hello Kitty with a cut-line that says, "Cute Outside and Angry Inside." The promotional copy featured on the YouthAIDS site explains why: "Hello Kitty is angry because every minute, somewhere in the world, a young person dies of HIV/AIDS."

That's a smart marketing move, as well as a worthy cause. Still, Kitty gets more flak than kudos among the counter-cultural types. But from a purely commercial point of view, it is hard to say the Hello Kitty brand has been really damaged in any kind of significant way by such spoofs in the artistic world. In fact, it can be argued that the Hello Kitty counter-culture at least keeps the character's name alive in the broader public consciousness. And five will get you 10, that Sanrio hasn't targeted radical feminists, lesbians and buff boys in its master marketing plan to keep the brand alive in the decades ahead. Sanrio's core global consumer base remains the young girls and teens and, in Asia, 20-something shoppers. There are other markets, to be sure, that Sanrio could and may go after, but this will never be the pierced-nose set.

PEACE ANGEL OR SATANIC PLAYTHING?

Aside from the satirists, others have co-opted the cat — keeping Hello Kitty's love of friendship, tea parties and cutie-pie values — to promote rather unconventional religious doctrines and New-Age philosophies. One site created by followers of Minami DaDa, a Japanese-Taiwanese woman with purportedly deep spiritual powers.[14] (Warning: Hello Kitty is about to enter another dimension in the time and space continuum.) It is a little unclear from the site what kind doctrine DaDa followers subscribe to, and what supernatural abilities or celestial insights DaDa has at her disposal. But the site is full of Hello Kitty accoutrement and there is an extended, though rambling, explanation of the similarities between Hello Kitty and DaDa, which for sheer entertainment value, is worth quoting at length. Herewith:

> Hello Kitty vs. Minami DaDa
>
> Hello Kitty is so popular in Taiwan and Japan. One time I watched the Hello Kitty stage show on TV, I found — Hello Kitty is a "Peace Angel"! When I type DaDa's story — "the Moon in the Back Mt.," I knew when DaDa came to this world, she asked God she's willing to come as long as the second world war stopped.
>
> When DaDa was born, the war stopped and Taiwan was recovered. I finally realized DaDa is just like Hello Kitty — she is a "Peace Angel"!
>
> DaDa's power is so unbelievable. Sometimes, even DaDa doesn't know her power. DaDa said: "When your magnetic field is the same with God's, she works automatically. The power is from God so though I don't know, I know the Almighty God takes care of every sentient being in the world." It's just like the one who create Hello Kitty — he gives the living energy to Hello Kitty and lets people who see Hello Kitty can get a lot of joy and happiness. DaDa is like Hello Kitty.

> DaDa hopes everyone who sees her can receive this gift from God — endless joy and the upgrade of spiritual power!
>
> DaDa is always like a little girl at the age of 15. DaDa wears Hello Kitty's rosette on her head, puts on Hello Kitty's slippers and wears Hello Kitty's Min-Nan clothes with her kind smile. People who see her will be very happy naturally. They can't tell why for DaDa's always gives people the invisible gift everywhere.

We wish DaDa and her followers bliss, and only mention the site to show just how far and wide Hello Kitty is bouncing around the global media. You won't find many performance artists and fringe devotional groups parsing through the subtext of Winnie the Pooh or Miffy. But there is something very powerful about Hello Kitty's image and the meanings others tend to draw from her or impose upon her.

For a fundamentalist Christian website called the KJOS Ministries in the U.S., Hello Kitty and Sanrio are doing the devil's work. Just check out this exchange on the comments page of the site.[15]

> Question: My (adult) son heard that McDonald's is about to introduce a new toy, "Hello Kitty." It is a paper white doll. He felt something in his spirit that there was something wrong with it, so he did a little research on the net and found it may be connected to some Japanese cult. We would like to know more but we are unable to get enough information. Can you help?
>
> Answer: Kitty and the rest of her "family" seem to be everywhere these days. The official "Hello Kitty" website introduces some of her family members. On its pretty pages, children meet all kinds of cute little characters and pagan symbols. A page titled "The Mystic Pandaba's Astrological Zone" introduces children to divination — one of the pagan practices God warns us to avoid.

If they choose to read their horoscope or write a question for the fortune teller, they could open the door to a growing interest in the timeless practices listed in Deuteronomy 18:9-12.

Finally, a page titled "The 'Social Communication' Business" features Shintaro Tsuji, President and CEO of the Sanrio Company:

> Sanrio Company promises to build character, tolerance, oneness and social skills — all in the context of Asian beliefs, traditions and values. These include superstitions, faith in a pantheism (a cosmic mind or energy infuses all things making everything sacred), and an emphasis on group thinking. None are compatible with Biblical faith. Nor are the pop-psychology and other dubious suggestions. God says, "Beware lest anyone cheat you through philosophy and empty deceit, according to the tradition of men, according to the basic principles of the world, and not according to Christ." Colossians 2:8

It seems the folks at KJOS think Kitty is leading young minds to the dark side. And truth be told, Sanrio probably could live with this sort of thing without too much harm to its brand. What it has a far tougher time living with are rip-off artists and product pirates that trash the Sanrio copyright, distribution contracts and so on, which siphons off huge profits.

CROSSING THE LINE

Takakura Nakamura and Atsuhiko Koizumi manage the legal department at Sanrio headquarters in central Tokyo. Middle-aged and world-weary, these two travel all over the globe in search of Hello Kitty knockoffs, and work with an array of outside legal teams, private detectives and local police authorities across Asia, the U.S. and Europe. For Sanrio, nailing every instance of counterfeiting on the Internet, the side streets of Shanghai or a toy distributor on the West Coast is a near impossible task, as Nakamura and Koizumi will readily attest. "We think we are probably losing about ¥100 billion ($800 million) in lost sales to the counterfeiters," lamented Nakamura.[16] And though there have been some widely publicized Hello Kitty raids across Asia, the con artists brazenly ignoring copyright laws just keep pouring out of the woodwork.

Without too much difficulty, infringement cases can be found on the web. Take the case of an online purveyor called DEN Trinity based in Hong Kong that sells air-powered guns designed to have the weight, feel and texture of high-powered, automatic pistols, rifles and battlefield weaponry. Three Hong Kong-based gun enthusiasts launched the site in the late 1990s. One of them, Clarence Lai, a professional gunsmith, decided to design an awesome-looking pistol called the "Hello Kitty Hi Capacity .45."[17] The handle is hot pink and smack dab in the middle of this lethal weapon is the queen of cute. Obviously, this isn't the sort of thing Sanrio's licensing and branding team would care to promote in any shape or form. Years ago, Tsuji issued a fiat that Hello Kitty would never be licensed to makers of any sort of weaponry, alcoholic beverages or any other type of product that harmed the brand. For some reason, though, Sanrio had no problem with the Hello Kitty vibrator, but that's another story.

Sanrio has employees in the U.S., Asia and Europe screening the Internet for inappropriate uses of the brand or knockoff products. Regarding the former, Hello Kitty sightings on Internet porn sites are a real headache. "It is very difficult to crack down on all the sites," said Nakamura, "we don't have the resources for that." When they do find cases of Hello Kitty being exploited in such a lascivious manner, a sharply worded letter from Sanrio's in-house or contracted legal teams in Tokyo and elsewhere can usually put a stop to it. Harder to crack down on are the counterfeiters, whose copycat-Sanrio products continue to grow in sophistication. Given Hello Kitty's global appeal and demand, the economic incentives are far too high for many unethical toy manufacturers and distributors to resist.

As far back as the mid-1970s, soon after Hello Kitty's debut, Sanrio started prosecuting copyright cases in courts from Madrid to Hong Kong. It has been a multi-decade campaign, but new outrages keep popping up left and right. In the U.S., it is usually easier to scare off those tempted to infringe upon Sanrio's copyrights and trademarks. For years, Sanrio has used the intellectual property law firm of Owen, Wickersham & Erickson to look out for its interests in the fast-growing U.S. market, where the company's stable of characters grosses about $100 million annually. For instance, one company in November of 2002 thought it could get away with selling a Hello Kitty look-alike inflatable jumper for kids. Sanrio lawyers shot off a threatening letter demanding that the company detail the number of products sold, the exact names and telephone numbers of its distributors, total revenues from the infringing product and an accounting of remaining inventory and so on. Sanrio prefers to end the matter with written assurance that the offender will see the light. But in outrageous cases, it will take the case to court and seek the disgorgement of profits, stiff statutory damages and attorney's fees.

HELLO KITTY INFORMANTS

Things are a lot trickier in Asian markets such as China, Taiwan and South Korea where the protection of intellectual property rights has been lax at best and in such places as Shanghai and Hong Kong, virtually non existent. Sanrio gets hit from all sides. Oftentimes, mom-and-pop toy makers will brazenly reverse engineer a Hello Kitty toothbrush or handbag and try to sell it at roadside stands in the region. In other instances, Sanrio's legitimate distributors and contract manufacturers will covertly extend the production run of an item beyond the agreed upon amount and then furtively dump the extra products into the market, while pocketing the additonal profits and skirting any royalty payments to the company. The problem has grown so out of hand, that Nakamura and Koizumi have a working network of private detectives around the region to detect instances of fraud.

One strategy is to use well-publicized raids of knock-off shops to get the word out that Sanrio is deadly serious about nailing counterfeiters. Back in 1999, for example, Sanrio's local distributor in Singapore, Rubber Band Enterprises, coordinated a raid with detectives from the Criminal Investigation Department's Intellectual Property Rights Warrant unit in the city-state's Chinatown district. They naturally tipped off the *The Straits Time* of Singapore and garnered some splashy coverage under the headline, *"Hello Kitty Pounces on Copy Cats."* Sanrio and its distributors also routinely take out full or half page ads that display all the major company characters such as Hello Kitty, My Melody, Bad Badtz-Maru, Pochacco and Kerokerokeroppi to remind consumers what the trademarked characters should look like. Such ads also display a "certificate of authorization" and urges consumers to look for the genuine articles at department stores.

Another approach that Sanrio employs is to use discounts and gifts to reward consumers who tip off the company when they discover copycat merchandise. One such notice featured Hello Kitty with a reminder to "help us track down imitation/ unlicensed Sanrio merchandise and you will be pleasantly rewarded." They are encouraged to fill out a coupon at the bottom of the ad and fire it off in the mail. The general idea is to turn Sanrio customers into informants. Of course, when all that fails there is always the public humiliation approach. As part of a settlement with seven retailers in Singapore, Sanrio demanded they foot the bill for a full-page apology in the local papers. At the top of the published apology are of course Hello Kitty, Pom Pom Purin, Pochacco and the others, looking as adorable as ever. Then those awful defilers of Sanrio products are listed by name as are their retail outlets and addresses. Then in bold type the perpetrators...

> Hereby Unreservedly Apologize to Sanrio Company, Ltd., of Japan, for infringing upon the copyrights and trademarks of Sanrio Company, Ltd., by selling products featuring one or more of the representations of Sanrio's Cartoon characters, namely HELLO KITTY, MY MELODY, LITTLE TWIN STARS, KEROKEROKEROPPI, POCHACCO and/or POM POM PURIN, without an appropriate license.[18]

CHINA SYNDROME

The mother of all counterfeiting markets, though, is China. It is bad enough that the Chinese toy market is saturated with look-alike Hello Kitty gadgets. On top of that, these pirated goods are also clearing Chinese customs and circulating all over the world. Hello Kitty hit Shanghai in the mid-1990s. The feline's image started appearing on stationery, mobile phones and eventually spread to thousands of products, ranging from electric toothbrushes to panties. Sanrio's local distributor, the Feng Cheng Group, had distribution deals in the year 2000 with just four major downtown department store chains such as the Pacific Department Store and Hymart. But Shanghai by that point was awash in Hello Kitty goods, an estimated 95% of which were cheaply priced rip-offs.[19] Regular sweeps through such shopping districts as the Yuyuan Garden area and roadside stalls all over the city kept yielding more and more of the stuff.

Even worse, mom-and-pop operations were cranking out an entire parallel universe of Hello Kitty goods and shipping the contraband all over the world. "The counterfeit goods

from China are finding their way to the U.S. and Africa,"
said Nakamura of Sanrio's legal team. "In Europe, there are
about two cases a week of pirated goods that get discovered
at customs." To net more of such goods at the border,
Sanrio's team spend a fair amount of time educating custom
officials about their various character brands and how to
look for knockoffs. They have printed up Sanrio's characters
roster in Chinese, Korean, Thai and all manner of languages
for custom officials. But with custom regimes casting a
gimlet eye on more pressing matters such as drug trafficking,
firearms, suicide bombers and weapons of mass destruction,
there is no need to wonder where the pressing matter of
halting counterfeit Hello Kitty nail clippers and Pochacco
lunchboxes comes in.

At Sanrio, Nakamura and his team have an assortment of
pirated Sanrio goods they have collected from around the world.
Some of the imitations are almost laughably poor in quality. To
the trained eye, it is easy to detect the fakes. Perhaps Kitty's
ribbon is on the wrong side, or a Sanrio character has been
teamed up inexplicably with a Warner Brothers' icon like Bugs
Bunny. Sometimes Sanrio is spelled "Scnria" in very tiny fine
print in a bid to avoid detection. Other giveaways are faulty bar
coding and fake registration numbers on the packaging. That the
fake goods were so obviously substandard used to ease the pain
of lost revenues somewhat. Sanrio could find some comfort in
the fact that most consumers would want the real thing. Trouble
is that the quality of ripped-off Sanrio products has improved
to such a point that it is getting harder and harder to tell the
difference. And don't even ask Nakamura about new emerging
pirating markets such as Russia.

EDUCATION MOMS

The legion of potential rip-off artists out there is a scary
prospect, but other dangers loom as well. Chief among them

is this: What if mothers, themselves, start to view Hello Kitty as an insidious force, a brain-draining influence on the kids. Sanrio has always assumed that young mothers in their late 20s and early 30s, who had encountered Hello Kitty during their pre-teen years, would carry with them a certain nostalgia factor. Without thinking twice, they would in due course shower their kids with Hello Kitty paraphernalia, if nothing less to make a certain kind of connection. That's understandable, even praiseworthy, in one sense. Part of being a parent after all is the imparting, the passing along of rituals, both sacred and profane.

But in another sense, aren't parents consciously or not, arbiters of good taste? Is it worth contemplating the following: Does a six-year-old draw more inspiration, imagination, an appreciation for the poetry of life from the kid-friendly baby talk of a purple dinosaur named Barney or the fictional wizardry and English boarding-school imagery of Harry Potter? Some might say, hey, you are comparing dinosaurs to boy wizards, you moron. Maybe so, but Barney is more about transmitting images of comfort and stability. The world is a happy people place. Elements of Harry Potter don't translate well with six-year-olds; in fact, they may well be baffled by some elements of the story or even rattled by the monsters. But should parents be more interested in projecting a super-sentimental world of simple colors and warm fuzzy things of Barney, of Hello Kitty of Cookie Monster — or exposing them to the complex, bizarre and scary visual language and symbolism of a Harry Potter or Disney's masterwork, *Fantasia*.

The answers to such questions will vary from family to family. And, truth be told, there is a certain snob appeal at work for a well-off Japanese mother in the rich enclave of Seijo, and her U.S. counterpart in Westchester County, New York, to prefer Harry Potter over Hello Kitty. They may not have given it much thought and may be subjected to the same herd-like instincts that drive so many to Sanrio's feline goddess.

But the lack of a cogent back story, a set of values and storylines give Hello Kitty a little more heft, all we are left with is a very simple fashion design. And it is slapped on virtually every product under God's provenance. In other words, Hello Kitty isn't about "social communication" in a deep and meaningful sense; it's about making money. There is nothing wrong with that, of course, and the same holds true for the brand caretakers and licensees of Harry Potter junk. Even so that has one design critic and mother asking whether Hello Kitty, in all her bubble-gum pink glory, is sending our kids a pretty cheap message, "a brazenly unadulterated endorsement of material culture she so faux-innocently represents."[20] While hardly shocking to advertising-bombarded parents or marketing pros, she pointed out:

> But to young children who represent the target audience for this sort of thing, it is indelible: Kitty is sweet and pink and pure. She unwraps sweet and pink and pure presents, and delivers sweet and pink and pure messages. (She herself never opens her mouth, though she dances quite a lot.) Kitty is cute. Kitty is pink. And Kitty is a designer. In the land of Kittydom, design is not only a persuasive tool, it is a psychological one: can design be a purveyor of happiness? Is this a worthy mission for children to consider, or a menacing one — one that thwarts their sense of reality, let alone design's capacity to engage that reality? Are we brainwashing an unsuspecting audience of preschoolers, who think design can save the world — or worse, suggesting to these young innocents that such a rescue is more likely to happen if there are cute pink kittens positioned at the front-lines of the design revolution?

All of this might strike Sanrio's design and branding teams as unduly harsh, a bit of inner-ear theorizing on the pedagogy of design and so much hot air. And yet, a product devoid of meaning does run the risk of, well, being pretty meaningless to a lot of parents who are ultimately the sheriffs in their kid's Toon Town. We will discuss this in greater detail in another chapter on why it's time to rethink the entire branding strategy for the moon-faced one. Right now, let's reflect, on how and why a cartoon character has touched off a massive culture war between cute and anti-cuties, has been the target of scathing satire, has been hijacked by perverts and otherworldly-types on the Internet and inspired bad poetry, cheap jokes about vibrators and has even served as hiding place for body parts. What does this in the end say about Hello Kitty? Or better yet, what does this say about us?

ENDNOTES

[1] Angel Lau, "Severed Head in Hello Kitty Doll," *South China Morning Post*, Oct. 10, 2000, News Section, 3.

[2] Clay Chandler, "Hello Kitty Murder Case Horrifies Hong Kong," *The Washington Post*, Dec. 9, 2000, A Section, A25.

[3] Lau, *South China Morning Post*, Oct. 10, 2000.

[4] Ali Lawlor, "Killers Were Close to Getting Away With It," *Hong Kong Mail*, Nov. 22, 2000, News Section, 3.

[5] Kitty Poems is at http://www.angelfire.com/hi/barbiesdead/kittypoems.html.

[6] Hello Kitty Has No Mouth can be found at http://www.queeg.com/hellokitty/.

[7] Ibid.

[8] Holly Myers, "Hello Kitty Finally Gets to Talk Back," *Los Angeles Times*, Oct. 25, 2002, Calendar.

[9] Denise Uyehara's site can be found at http://www.janet.org/~ebihara/uyehara/.

[10] Denise Uyehara, performance artist, personal interview, Dec. 2002.

[11] Big Bad Asia Mama can be found at http://www.bigbadchinesemama.com/.

[12] Ibid.

[13] Stuart Timmons, "Obituary of Jim Yousling", *LA Weekly* , Jan. 13, 1995.

[14] The Minami Dada page is at http://web1.makerweb.com.tw/afan/page/html-english/kitty-english.htm.

[15] The KJOS Ministries site is at http://www.crossroad.to/Q&A/Toys-Games/HelloKitty.htm.

[16] Takakura Nakamura, Sanrio's Deputy General Manager, Legal Department, personal interview, Tokyo, Nov. 15, 2002.

[17] The Den Trinity site and images of the Hello Kitty gun are at http://www.dentrinity.com/main.html.

[18] The authors obtained a copy of this apology from the legal department at Sanrio.

[19] Su Yanxian, "Hello Kitty's Popularity Leads to Copycats in City," *Shanghai Daily*, Jan. 12, 2000.

[20] Jessica Helfand, "The (Not-So) Secret Life of Hello Kitty and Other Tales," *Communication Arts,* December Advertising Annual 2002.

Chapter 7

Branding Hello Kitty

The phenomenal and global success of Hello Kitty poses some interesting questions about what drives consumer behavior, and how crazes suddenly explode on the scene. As fads go, the Hello-Kitty boom has some fascinating dimensions that should be of interest to marketing pros. For when it comes to parsing this cat's appeal, simple and obvious answers aren't always forthcoming. Hello Kitty defies much of the conventional wisdom about brand marketing. As a character good, she doesn't really have a detailed back story, a body of work (comics, film, whatever) that defines this cat in any meaningful sense. She is first and foremost a fashion icon that has been slapped onto all manner of consumer products. That said, she floats from culture to culture saying different things to different consumer segments. The evolution of Kitty throws up some interesting challenges to conventional marketing theory.

For instance, had Hello Kitty burst forth in the 1960s, the advertising and brand manager wizards of the day probably would have analyzed the success of the brand using the four Ps paradigm of marketing theory enshrined in the business textbooks of the day. The four Ps — as in product, price, place and promotion — were pretty much etched in stone for most marketing types back then, especially in the U.S., which was home to colossal consumer-product giants, chock full of business school-trained brand managers trying to transact with a mass market of buyers. Even today, the American Marketing Association clings to the rather dated and stale consensus view that "marketing is the process of planning and executing the conception, pricing, promotion and distribution of ideas, goods and services to create exchange and satisfy individual and organizational objectives."[1]

That all sounds so orderly and rational, as if selling stuff means calibrating the four Ps into just the right matrix to lure consumers. Voila! Welcome to a waterfront-organizing marketing theory, covering everything from a Toyota Lexus to a Cabbage Patch doll. Of course, few in the marketing world would subscribe to such a static view of selling things circa 2003. Obviously, price and value still matter greatly — but so do the emotional ties a consumer exhibits toward the brand, the whole raft of emotions one feels driving around in a 2004 Lexus RX330 or an eight-year-old's delight in expanding his Hot Wheels car collection. Marketing theorists during the 1990s started to think of brands and the whole process of selling in much more multifaceted terms. There is a lot more talk these days about relationship marketing, product meaning and consumer involvement with a brand. True, there is a lot of windbag analysis out there that veteran brand managers, creative directors and consumer-product executives — folks on the frontline of selling — would no doubt find grating.

Browse through the academic literature on marketing and you quickly run into books and articles that present such gripping titles as *The Ideology of Political Correctness and Its Effect on Brand Strategy* or the *Past, Present and Paradisal Future of Consumer Gender Identity*.[2] Oftentimes, such works dish out patently obvious observations (wow, our notions of masculinity and femininity have changed over time) or stabs-in-the-dark making obscure connections between consumer behavior laced with armchair psychoanalysis. Consider this virtual self-paradoy of what passes for marketing theory out there:

> Given that there is no essential essence to masculinity or femininity, and that gender is constructed by culture and language, then the emerging transformation, enhancement, and dilution of the culture that is occurring will continue to recontextualize the meanings of gender. In the new millennium, gender identity will likely reflect the creolization of signs and significations, a mixing of what is at hand, the old and the new, something that "just happens" in an emergent fashion. Given that gender is arbitrary and transcends the constraint of physical facts then in the new post-millennial society individuals will be able to pick and choose different gender schemes or chose not to care about gender at all. Gender identity will become a pastiche, a random collection of traits and roles and behaviors that lack familiar perceptible boundaries between men and women, a celebratory "medley" of potentialities.

While we may or may not be evolving into a global consumer class of cross-dressers, and we'd rather leave that for others to figure out back here in the real world of Ken and Barbie, this kind of analysis is no good to a copywriter trying to dream up a groin-tingling television campaign, featuring well-endowed blondes, aimed at convincing male consumers in their late 20s that it's cool to drink Coors or Budweiser. In all sorts of consumer-product categories, including those branded by Hello Kitty, gender differences do matter greatly. And for the foreseeable future, consumption will differ according to sex and so will the marketing strategies employed to sell them.

Another problem with such narrow analyses is that one variable like gender doesn't help explain how a fashion icon like Hello Kitty appeals to a vast and differentiated global youth culture. That is a real mind-bender, kind of a puzzle palace. And the truth is that the folks at Sanrio, including President Tsuji and his marketing team, can't really give you a comprehensive and credible reason as to why Hello Kitty worked, when so many of its other characters have faded from the scene. Of course, there is no assurance that Hello Kitty won't seem as passé to consumers in 2030 as that 1970s-vintage Smiley Button strikes us now, and Sanrio needs to be much more strategically minded about how it cares for and cultivates this brand in the years ahead. Unlike big consumer giants like Nestle, Procter & Gamble or Kao, Sanrio has never taken a very scientific approach to the art of selling. (The big exception is the Sanrio team in the U.S., which has used market research to shape its strategy, owing to the unfamiliarity of the market by top executives in Tokyo.) Sanrio has always relied on the gut instincts of its founder — and his instincts haven't been too shabby.

Keeping Hello Kitty alive and well will demand some pretty imaginative marketing strategies that draw from the bleeding edge of marketing theory, especially as it pertains to children. We will offer some specific suggestions elsewhere in the book. But here we hope to dwell on how the success of Hello Kitty reveals just how intellectually bankrupt traditional marketing theory has become in telling us much about why people — in decidedly different economies and cultures, go ga-ga over such a simple and sentimental image, whose exact appeal is tough to pin down. The 4 Ps just don't come close to explaining the evolution of a global craze.

SHIFTING PARADIGMS

What makes Kitty so intriguing is that she projects entirely different meanings depending on the consumer. A Japanese teen finds emotional comfort in Hello Kitty artifacts, while a 20-something single woman in New York may like the feline as a display of whimsical camp. Figuring out what makes brands click, how they migrate across borders and appeal to widely divergent demographic groups, has long been the Holy Grail for market researchers. And the whole field has become a lot more sophisticated in gathering and manipulating raw sales data, census numbers and the like. It is also increasingly drawing upon the worlds of cultural anthropology and cognitive psychology.

Even new and emerging interdisciplinary fields that fall under the rubric of complexity or network theories may be of use to modern marketers and help shed some light on the fabled feline. The devotees of such schools of thought view human society as networks in which a few random connections can quickly multiply into something much larger. In the context of marketing, that could be an overnight mania for a certain product or, conversely, it could be a bit of negative publicity that swirls into a sandstorm and does severe damage to a brand in ways quite unforeseen. Back in 1987, James Gleick penned a book called *Chaos: Making A New Science*, which popularized complexity theory. He asked his readers to imagine the flapping of a butterfly's wings in China setting off a chain of events and outcomes that somehow caused a blizzard thousands of miles away in Chicago.[3] The basic idea is that all sorts of ecosystems — be they solar systems, the human brain or the market for Hello Kitty G-strings often add up to much more than the sum of their parts. You can't predict their behavior or evolution based on one set of variables that fit nicely into a linear line of thinking. In these environments, the expected cause and effect don't always play out as one would think. Hello Kitty, for instance, became a global sensation nearly two decades after its launch in 1974 because a unique culmination of forces — mostly outside the direct management control of Sanrio — that suddenly expanded brand awareness exponentially and sparked a craze.

Other writers such as Malcolm Gladwell have echoed such academic musings. In his book, *The Tipping Point: How Little Things Can Make a Big Difference,*[4] Gladwell sought a unifying theory for an array of social phenomena from the sudden drop in New York's stubbornly high crime rate in the mid-1990s to how television shows such as *Sesame Street* spawn literacy among preschool kids. The phrase, "tipping point" is borrowed from the world of epidemiology, where change, and the pace of change, can happen suddenly and with incredible force. As Gladwell explained:

> *The Tipping Point* is about change. In particular, it's a book that presents a new way of understanding why change often happens as quickly and as unexpectedly as it does. How does a novel written by an unknown author end up as a national bestseller? Why do teens smoke in greater and greater numbers, when every single person in the country knows that cigarettes kill? Why is word-of-mouth so powerful? What makes TV shows like *Sesame Street* so good at teaching kids how to read? I think the answer to all those questions is the same. It's that ideas and behavior and messages and products sometimes behave just like outbreaks of infectious disease. They are social epidemics.[5]

In the case of Hello Kitty, word-of-mouth networks among the character's fanatical following certainly played a big role. They eventually built upon one another and expanded at a ferocious rate through the 1990s in Japan. The tipping point came when several Japanese pop divas mentioned in interviews that they had collected a pile of Hello Kitty artifacts. By the end of 1990s and early into this decade, this "epidemic" had spread to Hong Kong, South Korea, Taiwan and Singapore. Now, it appears to be reaching another tipping point in the U.S., though it is a little hard to say with precision. The upshot here is that the marketing team at Sanrio, though it promotes Hello Kitty accoutrement wherever and whenever it can, probably couldn't write a can't-miss marketing plan that could duplicate the success of Hello Kitty and the worldwide embrace of the brand. Somewhere along the way, Hello Kitty as a brand took on a life of its own. In short, you can't really predict with any certainty what separates the super hits from the duds. (Though that won't stop chief executives and movie producers from trying should they stumble on a runaway hit of their own.)

EMOTIONAL LOYALTY

It's also worth noting that tipping points and other network effects can savage a brand in unexpected ways. Consider the case of New Coke, perhaps one of the greatest marketing fiascos of all time. Back in 1985, Coca-Cola launched a reformulated version of its soft drink in a classic bit of brand extension. There must have been a high degree of comfort level at the company's Atlanta headquarters ahead of the launch. After all, Coca-Cola employed some of the best marketing minds on the planet. And they also did their spadework. According to one study of the debacle, the company spent a cool $4 million on market research and interviewed somewhere in the neighborhood of 200,000 consumers.[6] (That's about twice the population of a small midwestern town like Peoria.) What's more, New Coke seemed to be blowing away old Coke in taste tests (63% to 37%) and only 10% or so had strong feelings against the soft-drink upgrade.[7]

Having spent enormous resources on due diligence, Coca-Cola hit the button and rolled out New Coke — and it touched off a firestorm among the old Coke crowd that knocked the company back on its hind side. They trashed New Coke at every opportunity and once the business press caught on and started covering the story, the level of negative feelings quickly spread among the Coca-Cola drinking population, which is to say a big chunk of rich-world consumers. The company did its best to defuse the uproar, by later splitting its franchise product into New Coke and Coca-Cola Classic. But by 1990, New Coke was pretty much dead in the water. Coca-Cola burned through an estimated $48 million in marketing costs and strained its credibility with its most loyal consumers. According to one study of the subject, one lesson drawn from the flop is this:

> The New Coke experience provides a glimpse into the strong emotional undercurrents of powerful brands. Be it with Coca-Cola, Nike or Harley Davidson, some loyal consumers experience a relationship that goes well beyond the fulfillment of a functional need. They are militant in their commitment to their brand: creating positive word of mouth for the brand, experiencing the product to its fullest and, if defrauded, launching frontal attacks on the company. In many ways, brand managers act as chaperones of these relationships, trying to strike a difficult balance between commitment to the core of the franchise and the desire to reach out to new segments.[8]

In the case of the rebellion against New Coke, there seemed to be a backlash against the perceived defilement of a product that had been unaltered over many generations, save for packaging. In this sense, Coke seems deeply rooted to a feeling of nostalgia among its most zealous consumers. On a more positive note, the Nike swoosh mark conjures up feeling about athleticism among male Americans or perhaps feelings of aspiration. After all, its pitchmen over the years have been such sports mega-stars as Michael Jordan and Tiger Woods. Computer-maker Apple appeals to anti-conformists, a carefully cultivated emotional bond cemented by the famous "1984" and "Think Different" campaigns.

The core issue here: The needs of emotionally engaged consumers toward a brand have to be treated with great delicacy and cultivated on a continuing basis. Your best customers will be the most expressive and, depending on the circumstances, that means plenty of tailwinds or headwinds in a brand's development. One big advantage for Hello Kitty is the enormous emotional energy she generates not just among young girls but older ones as well — and across much of Asia and the U.S. That creates a pretty big and instant following for Sanrio's aggressive brand extension strategy into some 22,000 different products from toy vacuum cleaners to high-end luxury goods. It is true that other brands have morphed into entirely different product lines. Think of Giorgio Armani and prescription eyeglasses and Swiss Army wristwatches. But character goods such as Hello Kitty, not to mention Mickey Mouse and Snoopy seem to allow for a far greater range of product extensions. Some marketing experts speak of the so-called "brand halo" effect, in which a critical mass of emotionally charged and exceedingly loyal fans follow a brand religiously from product to product. Sanrio has been blessed by such a group. Other companies would die for such an advantage.

THE WAY OF JAPAN

Perhaps it is worth noting how Japanese marketing approaches have evolved over time. Though Hello Kitty, as her story goes, hails from England, her marketing overlords at Sanrio have been primarily Japanese executives at least until the 1990s when the company started to hire local talent in overseas markets such as the U.S. Japanese companies as a rule have always been more interested in market share than profits and shareholder returns, though that is beginning to change. A big reason for that is the nature of Japanese corporate finance. For decades, companies and their primary lenders cemented business ties by buying equity in each other. Companies, for the most part, could count on ample and cheap credit from their primary lenders and rely less on the equity market, which in the U.S. tends to be a very stern taskmaster; outfits that don't deliver quarterly profits, steady stock appreciation and dividend payments often see their share prices take a beating. Not so in Japan.

What this meant in practice is that Japanese automakers and consumer electronics makers often took a very long-term approach toward marketing. During Japan's high-speed growth years from the double-digit pace of the 1960s to the bubbly excesses of the 1980s, Japanese companies were extremely adept at quickly becoming the market leader on price, and then relentlessly upgrading and differentiating their product on functionality and quality. Not surprisingly, particularly against weak competitors in the U.S., a number of Japanese multinationals clawed their way up the product food chain and amassed monster market share, if not always stellar profits, along the way. One study on the essential attributes of the Japan way of marketing put it this way:

> A popular samurai tactic was to 'strike at the corners.' It was believed that if the corners were overthrown, the spirit of the whole body would be overthrown. Then one should follow up the attack, when the corners have collapsed. This strategy has been used in various industries including automobiles, semiconductors and consumer electronics. The Japanese are masters of looking for and exploiting differences in the total market. These strategies create competitive gaps that will either cause brand-switching to occur or that will increase industry market potential in industries with untapped growth potential.[9]

A second characteristic, and more apt to the success of Hello Kitty, is that Japanese advertising strategies have always stressed the holistic nature of their products — in other words not just the particular function of a car or toy, but its intangible components. As we shall see, American marketers are increasingly sensitive to the feelings a product evokes to consumers and that now factors heavily into their marketing strategies. But it is fair to say that Japanese marketers were on to this a long time ago. Naturally, Sanrio's top executives want to make yen, truckloads of it. But it is also true, particularly of the founder Tsuji, that Hello Kitty and the company's cast of characters are in the business of social communication, the transmission of idealized images of cuteness and comfort to make everyday life a tad brighter. That may seem trite to more cynically minded types, but it is hard to doubt the sincerity of Sanrio's upper management on this score. And even if you do, you can't argue with the results.

ICON OF INNOCENCE

So when thinking about Hello Kitty, the emotional ties to the brand are considerable. One only has to think of the mob that stormed the McDonald's in Singapore that had a Hello Kitty promotion back in the year 2000. Or consider the scores of Internet sites that tie together Hello Kitty's most devout fans. But what is the exact nature of the emotional bond tethering consumers to such a simple character? What psychological needs does this cat sate? To get a satisfactory answer, some marketing specialists think it pays to delve a little more deeply into such notions as modern mythology and the contours of what is often called the "Image Economy" — as opposed to the economy of goods and services.

In his book *Building Brands & Believers*, verteran international advertising executive, Kent Wertime, described how commercial images virtually bombard our every waking moment with the message to buy, certainly, but offering deeper meanings as well:

> The impact of the Image Economy, however, is more than just financial. Brands and personalities are fixtures

and talking points in societies all over the world. Human fascination with images ensures that the content of the Image Economy influences contemporary societies. The influence begins with the ubiquity of commercial images today. The Image Economy touches people from the second they wake up until the time they go to sleep. Billboards and shop signs expose them to brand names and sales pitches. Packaging for product communicates values and personalities of the products. The media blast out star-powered entertainment and advertising. According to some studies, people are bombarded with over 2,000 messages in this manner every day.[10]

That's all well and good, but how to create brands that stand out in the great cacophony of images that overwhelm us each and every day? Wertime drew inspiration from Carl Jung's theory of the "collective unconscious" in which arche-types, primal forms, such as the Mother Goddess and Hero have common meaning across large social groups. He argued that whether marketers realized it or not, such primordial symbols were the DNA of communications. And clever marketers could fashion a kind of modern mythology to bolster their brands and sell stuff. He identified 12 such modern variations including the Siren (in other words, sex sells), the Hero and Anti-Hero, Mother Goddess, Wise Man and so on. According to Wertime, Hello Kitty falls under the commercial archetype of Mother Goddess, given that she "represents the purity in all of us — the need to hold certain things sacred and undefiled," and that powerful connection has cemented with consumers.[11]

Those consumers, at least their first encounter with Hello Kitty, tend to be about three-feet tall with unique psychological needs of their own. Not surprisingly, there is a pretty extensive sub-genre of marketing theory that explores selling goods to kids. Some recent works on the subject have delved into the key cognitive stages of kids from infancy to late adolescence to give companies clues and guidance into how to design and market their brands. One of the more comprehensive guides to the psychology of marketing to kids is a 1997 book by Dan S. Acuff and Robert H. Reiher, two kid-marketing consultants, entitled appropriately enough as, *What Kids Buy and Why*.[12] In many ways it is quite relevant to our understanding of the success of the Hello Kitty brand.

FROM BARBIE TO BEAVIS AND BUTT-HEAD

One of the advantages of such a broad waterfront of Hello Kitty products is that there is something out there to meet the emotional and functional needs of just about every age group of female consumers. Take the critical first three years of life, which Acuff and Reiher dub the age of dependency and exploration. Of course, there is no mystery as to what the basic needs of an infant are — a sense of emotional security and plenty of sensory stimulation to kick-start neural development and language ability. The other obvious point is that two-year olds generally don't carry around a lot of cash and credit cards and make their own purchasing decisions at Toys 'R' Us. Parents call the shots here — and thus, marketers must play to them in a critical sense by appealing to their sense of nostalgia if their brands have been around long enough or perhaps stress the educational or developmental value of their product. It doesn't take much to tap into the normal parental anxiety that their little one would not have a shot at being the next Mozart without a full assortment of Fisher-Price and Playskool toys to stimulate the brain.

Hello Kitty dolls, stickers, notebooks and the like, don't have an obvious educational edge nor do parents in Japan or the U.S. associate the brand with learning. (This is perhaps a missed opportunity that will be explored later.) But Hello Kitty's warm and simple image and assortment of stuffed animal products do play to another need — the desire to hold and touch simple, non-threatening and nurturing characters.

Disney, of course, has long been the master of this sort of market niche. The nostalgic power of its decades-long brands such as Mickey Mouse and Winnie the Pooh needs no elaborating. The same holds true for Sesame Street icons such as Big Bird. And more recent brands such as Cabbage Patch Kids and Beanie Babies have also plugged into this arena with great effect. As kids get older they prefer more ironic characters such as Garfield and Ren & Stimpy. But at this stage it's best for the design to be non-threatening and simple. It also helps if your character is an animal with a soft and rounded design. And Hello Kitty certain fits the bill. Acuff and Reiher cite two pieces of research that should be of interest to kid marketers:

> Children are fascinated by and attracted to animals of all kinds. In fact, some research has shown that as much as 80% of children's dream content is of animals up to about the age of six. It appears that through animal dreams children work on the resolution of a variety of issues and fears they are dealing with in their young lives. Given the safety and nurturing needs of this age, characters like Big Bird and Barney are designed to be round and nurturing and safe. Regarding roundness, research has proven that as early as 18 months of age, children identify crooked, jagged lines as 'bad guys' or things that could hurt you, and round curving lines as being good guys and safe.[13]

A safe and simple design for toddlers as well as slightly older kids is critical for another reason: In highly litigious economies such as the U.S., toy makers who are lambasted by special interest groups about the alleged risks of their products can face all sorts of ugly publicity if their product is implicated in some sort of child injury or fatality. Groups such as National Association of State Public Interest Research Groups publish an annual list of hazardous toys entitled "Trouble in Toyland." It is usually released toward the end of the year, just ahead of the all-critical Christmas toy-purchasing season to attract maximum media attention.[14] No toy maker wants that kind of publicity and Sanrio would be wise to read the fine print on the U.S. Child Safety Protection Act of 1994, which requires specific warnings on toys with small parts that pose choking hazards, or some other threat, to children under the age of six. Fairly or unfairly, in late 2002, three Sanrio products showed up on the list. The three toys at issue included a Hello Kitty five-piece stamp set and Hello Kitty Super Bouncy Ball, which the group said lacked choking hazard warnings. The third product was pink, glitter nail polish that the group maintained included a chemical component that can create skin and eye irritation. Putting aside the credibility of the charges, this kind of publicity if it continues year after year can do serious damage to a character good and should be avoided at all cost.

CABBAGE KIDS VS. POWER RANGERS

The next important age cohort is the three- to seven-year-old group. Nurturing, feeling secure and that sort of thing are still important, of course. But the children start to develop other needs such as stimulation and play, a bit more autonomy at times. They tend to be more impulsive and self-centered. And they often like to accumulate or collect variations of a particular brand. Some important gender differences also start to emerge. Looking at two big mega-hits of the 1990s, Cabbage Patch Kids and Power Rangers, Acuff and Reiher identified key characteristics that drove the success of these brands, with girls and boys, respectively. Starting with the Cabbage Patch products, there is an essential nurturing quality at work here. The dolls' broad and dimpled features are cute and babyish. Their outstretched arms can be interpreted as comforting or needy, so a young girl can either baby the dolls or somehow feel mothered by them, the authors pointed out.

There is also what they call a "like me" identification process going on, in which a girl views a doll as a young child just about her age. Both these factors, by the way, are strong selling points for Hello Kitty, too. Finally, the fact that all the Cabbage Patch Kids have their own look, name and unique identity, often satisfy the "this is mine" need common in this age group. Noted Acuff and Reiher: "The three-through-seven-year-old stage of development is very much an egocentric period: a greater sense of mine due to the personalization of these dolls lends them greater appeal." Power Rangers appeals to boys because of factors such as hero identification, control, physical power, dark-side appeal and special effects. Given all that, it's not hard to see why most Hello Kitty products appeal to women, though the cat does have a campy following in the gay community.

Another key thing for companies targeting a younger audience with character-goods driven products is that children in most advanced markets have passion for collecting. Smart toy companies have learned this early on and so did Sanrio. Hello Kitty is far from a solo act. She has a twin sister named Mimmy, who is "shy, and a bit of a homebody, she wears a ribbon on her right ear so people can tell her and Kitty apart," according to Sanrio. Her papa, George White is a little absentminded, while mother Mary White is famous for her apple pie. Hello Kitty also has bright and cheerful friends such as Cathy, a "quiet, gentle little bunny girl" and Jodie, a "dog with a noggin for knowledge."

No secret here. The bigger Hello Kitty's extended family, the more varied the brand extension and sales opportunities. But it is also true that Hello Kitty, though her character is far from fully developed, sends out reassuring messages to young girls about the importance of families and having friends. In other words, building out the product line has the double advantage of strengthening the emotional bond with the character. There are similar examples of this strategy in Japan, which may not be surprising given the focus on group harmony. Interestingly enough, the fabled Ultraman started out as a lone superhero back in the 1960s when Tsuburaya Productions launched the action figure in a television costume drama. The plot lines were fairly simple: Meet monster, fight monster, kick butt and live on for another week and another adventure. But as each year passed, new ultra-brothers were introduced as well as parents. According to one writer, two forces were at work:

> The commercial advantages of this big happy family of Ultramen, in terms of dolls, suits, stickers and so on, are obvious. But it is probably also fair to say that Ultraman was originally modeled on a solitary Superman and developed his family because filial loyalty, fraternal solidarity, camaraderie and teamwork were found to have more appeal for Japanese children than the struggles of a lone individual.[15]

Of course, no matter how successful a character good becomes, at some point, usually around age 12 or so, it's time to leave childish things in the toy box and get on with being a teenager. In the U.S., Hello Kitty fanatics start to die out right about that age. In Japan, however, girls don't feel such peer pressure and remaining cute and childish well into adult life isn't all that unusual. In the West, though, there is sometimes a backlash against the childhood toy icons. In the U.S., there were some reported cases of actors dressed up as Barney getting physically harassed during promotions in shopping malls.[16] And just as anti-Hello Kitty art and websites have sprouted up all over the Internet, it is also true for fabled pieces of Americana such as Barbie. One review of the controversy swirling around the plastic princess of American sexuality boiled down her detractors into two groups: "The Barbie is the face of wicked American imperialism camp; and the Barbie corrupts young girls with shallow messages that promote style over substance lot."[17]

CONSUMUTOPIA

Interestingly enough, even the rarified academic world of cultural anthropology has plenty to teach about the marketing of cuteness, particularly in Japan. It's amazing how many times this cat and Sanrio show up in academic literature. Perhaps one reason is that cute sentiments and objects are such a pervasive part of the visual landscape of urban and consumer-driven Japan. As discussed earlier in this book, cuteness operates on several levels. Cuteness can be used to express relations in a social hierarchy. To men, cute, innocent and helpless women are seen as less threatening than assertive ones. It can also be an expression of femininity to attract men, or subtly exploit them. For our purposes, though, the essential point is that cuteness can be packaged, turned into a commodity and sold for a profit. In that sense, Sanrio really sells cuteness packaged in the form of various character goods and then slapped onto all manner of products.

One of the more interesting takes on Hello Kitty's appeal comes from Brian J. McVeigh, the chairman of Cultural and Women's Studies Department at Tokyo Jogakkan College. Writing for the *Journal of Material Culture* in 2000,[18] he identified five variables as the primary underpinning to the Hello Kitty mania: a unifying leitmotif, accessibility, ubiquity, projectability and contagious desire. The first three concepts aren't all that hard to get your head around. Slapping the same moon-faced, ribbon-festooned, cute-as-button feline on some 22,000 products makes a lot of economic sense from Sanrio's point of view. McVeigh noted that Sanrio gets royalties of about 3% every time a licensed company anywhere in the world sells a Hello Kitty whatever. Also, a big chunk of earnings, perhaps one-third, come from licensing fees. That certainly also guarantees that the image will be ubiquitous and accessible, and though the functionality of a Hello Kitty toothbrush and toaster may differ, the image is the same more or less.

What makes the brand particularly interesting, though, is that Sanrio characters often make their big debut on some product, be it a lunch pail or bed sheets. Other character goods tend to work in the other direction, first being developed in comic strips and films and then migrating over into merchandise sales like so many of the Disney characters. Sanrio characters are thus rather vague and loosely defined, which in turn actually broadens their appeal. As McVeigh described it: "Such a lack of embellishment provides carte blanche for whatever an individual feels, and it is this very impreciseness, indeterminateness, and vagueness that work to the advantage of the business concerns behind Hello Kitty: her plainness characterizes her as a cryptic symbol waiting to be interpreted and filled in with meanings."[19] She kind of functions like a mirror, embodying cuteness to girls, coolness to young women and camp or nostalgia to older female consumers. The image's ability to incite desire, be it a feeling of childhood comfort or a small bit of escapism from the drudgery of everyday life, makes Hello Kitty somewhat contagious. Who knows how long all this will last, but this blissful state between Sanrio and its consumer base could be dubbed a kind of consumutopia.

Add it all up and it's clear that cuteness and cute characters can help cast a more flattering light on the whole calculating side of capitalism — creating or exploiting consumer desires to trigger transactions and allow companies to turn a profit, the bigger the better. In Japan, cute cartoon characters are also used with great effect by the government to instruct the public about traffic safety and to discourage the groping of teenage girls on trains. In that sense, McVeigh noted:

> Hello Kitty teaches us that what we have in our daily life is not a stern Big Brother from the monolithic state office of propaganda demanding blind obedience, but rather countless little sisters — or more accurately in the case of Hello Kitty, little critters — dispatched by

corporate culture who kindly persuade (but not necessarily convince us) to consume. There is no conspiracy
here to control the masses through hedonistic consumption, but there is an ideology — or set of ideologies
to be more exact — of capital accumulation, profit-
taking, and expanding market share, all given a powerful
aesthetic spin.[20]

Another example of anthropology being applied to
marketing is embodied in the work of such firms as Envirosell
in New York. Its founder Paco Underhill, a former urban
geographer, has been consulted by McDonald's, Starbucks
and Blockbuster about how to improve their store
environments to move more products and keep consumers
coming back for more. Similar to the kind of field research an
anthropologist might do, Underhill and his team set up a
series of video cameras at a test store to chronicle the every
move and glance of shoppers. He then prepared detailed
reports for his clients with suggestions for improved store
design and product placement. When it came to retail
environment for kids, he suggested making sure the product
is easily accessible to kids. "If it's within their reach, they
will touch it, and if they touch it there's at least a chance that
Mom or Dad will relent and buy it (Dad especially)," noted
Underhill.[21]

SUSTAINING THE CRAZE

Let's shift gears and examine some case studies of brands
similar to Hello Kitty as well as relationship marketing, the
emotional bonds between brand and buyer, and the different
meanings a product can come to represent. Consider the
extraordinary story of Beanie Babies, which were first launched
in 1993 by Ty Inc. based in the U.S. By the mid-1990s, these
soft, cuddly stuffed animals had touched off a mania when
product shortages started occurring, especially during the

Christmas season. The media started to write about the brand, and that intensified demand. And just like Hello Kitty, a McDonald's product tie-in brought Beanie Babies international notoriety. The fastfood giant saw its five-week supply of Teenie Beanies, a miniaturized version of the Beanie Babies, that were part of a Happy Meal promotion, disappear in about one week's time. Meanwhile, a huge and vast secondary market for Beanie Babies emerged at toy exhibitions and on the Internet. Some of the more sought-after Beanie Babies characters, such as Peanut and Royal Blue Elephant, fetched thousands of dollars.

When two marketing professors analyzed the Beanie Baby phenomenon in the year 2000, they identified a number of attributes that worked to drive the brand, with precious little advertising and marketing support from Ty. Like Hello Kitty, the network effects of rapid word-of-mouth communication and media coverage of the Beanie craze worked like magic. Although a relatively new brand, Beanie Baby did conjure up nostalgic feelings among adults, who bought the toys for the kids or themselves. Ty's product designers deserve a great deal of credit for pulling that off. For instance:

> Several of the animals have also been designed with names and personalities Baby Boomer parents will associate with favorite childhood characters such as "Spot, the Black and White Dog," which is purported to have been named after the dog in "Dick, Jane and Sally" readers. "Magic the Dragon" is named to provide a reminder of the Peter, Paul and Mary song, "Puff the Magic Dragon." A tie-dyed series of BBs includes "Garcia the Bear," which shares the same birth date as Grateful Dead bandleader Jerry Garcia.[22]

Another similarity to Hello Kitty is that Beanie Babies have been personified by their creators at Ty. Each stuffed animal has a unique name, birthday and comes with a short poem. (It goes without saying, that having a wide product line of

Beanie Babies makes them collectible.) The verse accompanying a picture of Baby Boy the Bear goes something like this:

> *"Ten little fingers, ten little toes*
> *A tuft of hair, a button nose*
> *This healthy, bouncing baby boy*
> *Will bring you love and lots of joy."*

Ty has also been clever in engineering uniqueness into the brand. The company has been disciplined about keeping tight control over distribution and retiring certain styles to create scarcity and keep the mystique of the product. Sanrio has caught on to that tactic of using limited product runs to spur collecting behavior and repeat purchases. Another advantage is that Beanie Baby followers tend to be a highly involved consumer and interested in interacting with other like-minded souls, or relaying their passion for the product to others. There is an aesthetic appeal to the brand. They are pleasant to hold and squeeze and are flexible and plush. Also, as students of the brand point out, Ty takes toy design very seriously and modifies its characters, in some instances, after getting feedback from its consumers.

As with Hello Kitty, the Beanie Baby line has drawn its share of copycats and rip-off artists. While the company has been pretty religious about cracking down on the knockoffs to jealously guard the image for quality of the Beanie Baby line, it has been more lenient about the myriad websites that have cropped up as forums for production information, transactions in the secondary market and so on. Sanrio, too, understands the advantage of having a big and shared online community that keeps the brand alive in chat rooms. Even satirical Hello Kitty websites are a plus in that regard. Another link between Hello Kitty and Beanie Baby is that both brands have been positioned as the ideal gift and in times of product scarcity that role is only enhanced. In Japan's gift-giving happy culture, Hello Kitty stationery, towels and other knick-knacks are typically priced under ¥1,000, or about $8. Beanie Babies were priced at about $5 when they came on the scene and early on were very popular Christmas stocking stuffers.

Every character-goods brand will have its own dynamics; there is simply no denying that. And the attributes that drive Beanie Baby or Hello Kitty may not necessarily work elsewhere. One famous case in Japan is the short-lived boom involving an egg-shaped mobile electronic pet that spread across Asia. Like Hello Kitty, Tamagotchi mania owed much to Japan's cult of cuteness. After all, the toy was a digital pet chick that demanded constant care and feeding from its owner. Soon after its launch in late 1996, the Japanese toymaker Bandai Co. realized it had a major hit on its hand. Going for about $16 a piece, consumers mobbed Japanese stories to nab the must-have toy sensation. Some were going for $400 on the black market. Behind all the hysteria was a device that simulates the growth of a tiny chicken in a small liquid-crystal display hanging from a two-inch-long, egg-shaped plastic key chain. When you clicked it on, an image of a baby chick appeared. During its average 10-day life span — the chick grows the equivalent of a year every day — it will peep up a storm when it's lonely, when it's hungry, or when it has left little digital droppings in its wake. The chick's owner must then press the appropriate buttons to feed or clean the little thing.

If they are well cared for, the critters will eventually evolve into thriving and lovable characters. "It makes me feel like I'm a mother raising a child," a 24-year old, single woman told one magazine, adding, "I leave it with my mother for baby-sitting when I can't carry it with me."[23] But you have one sick chick on your hands if a feeding is missed. If you're really negligent, a ghostly Tamagotchi appears. At first, the biggest challenge facing Bandai was to keep its factories fired up to meet the rapacious demand. In early 1997, Bandai already had its factory in China on a 24-hour production schedule and was sending the gizmos to Japanese toy stores by air freight to feed the frenzy. Even so, it was not enough and frustrated customers deluged Bandai's home page on the Internet, while its Tokyo headquarters received 5,000 telephone calls a day. Retailers even resorted to lotteries to allocate their scarce stock. By 1998, Bandai had cranked up production around Asia into overdrive — but then suddenly the whole fad passed away with barely a peep, peep, peep. Demand fell off a cliff, while inventory costs for unsold Tamagotchi toys hit the stratosphere. As a result of that miscall and other problems, Bandai ended up taking a $16 million loss for its fiscal year that ended in March of 1999.[24]

In sum, Hello Kitty and other product crazes sometimes materialize out of nowhere. There are no such things as sure-fire hits. Yet sustaining a craze can and should be the result of careful and creative market planning. Hello Kitty offers some rich insights because of the cute power of the brand, its broad global appeal and unique ability to say so many things to so many diverse groups. Unlocking the secrets of this cat's success requires something more than just analyzing the business school saw about product, price, place and promotion. It also requires some imaginative thinking when the passion starts to cool, as it inevitably does, toward the product. We will explore just what sort of marketing tactics Sanrio should explore to make sure Hello Kitty keeps her groove for many years to come.

ENDNOTES

[1] Christian Gronroos, "From Marketing Mix to Relationship Marketing — Towards a Paradigm Shift in Marketing," *Management Decision*, Volume 35, (1997): 322-339.

[2] Jacqueline J. Kacen, "Girrl Power and Boyyy Nature: The Past, Present and Paradisal Future of Consumer Gender Identity," Marketing Intelligence & Planning, Volume 18, Issue 6/7 (2000): 345-355.

[3] James Gleick, *Chaos: Making a New Science* (New York: Viking Press, 1987).

[4] Malcolm Gladwell, *The Tipping Point: How Little Things Can Make a Big Difference* (New York: Little Brown & Company, 2000).

[5] "Interview with Malcolm Gladwell," Jan. 26, 2003. Transcript on the web at http://www.bookbrowse.com/index.cfm?page=author&authorID=392&view=Interview.

[6] Horacio D. Rozanski, Allen G. Baum, and Bradley T. Wolfsen, "Brand Zealots: Realizing the Full Value of Emotional Brand Loyalty," *Strategy + Business*, Fourth Quarter 1999, Booz Allen Hamilton Inc.

[7] Ibid.

[8] Ibid.

[9] Alain Genestre, Paul Herbig, Alan T. Shao, "What Does Marketing Really Mean to the Japanese," *Marketing Intelligence and Planning*, Volume 13, 1995.

[10] Kent Wertime, Building Brands & Believers: How to Connect with Consumers Using Archetypes, (Singapore: John Wiley & Sons (Asia) Pte. Ltd., 2002), 7.

[11] Ibid., 181.

[12] Dan S. Acuff, PhD., with Robert H. Reiher PhD, *What Kids Buy and Why: The Psychology of Marketing to Kids* (New York: The Free Press, New York, 1997).

[13] Ibid., 46.

[14] The National Association of State Public Interest Research Groups' annual hazardous toy list can be found at: http://toysafety.net/index.html.

[15] Tom Gil, *The World of Japanese Popular Culture: Gender, Shifting Boundaries and Global Cultures*, ed., D.P. Martinez (Cambridge, U.K., Cambridge University Press, 1998).

[16] Acuff and Reiher, 69.

[17] "Life in Plastic," *The Economist*, Dec. 21, 2002.

[18] Brian J. McVeigh, "How Hello Kitty Commodifies The Cute, Cool and Camp: Consumutopia versus Control in Japan," *Journal of Material Culture*, 2002, Vol. 5(2): 225-245.

[19] Ibid., 242.

[20] Ibid.

[21] Paco Underhill, "*Why We Buy: The Science of Shopping*," Touchstone, New York, 1999, 144.

[22] Rebecca J. Morris, and Charles L. Martin, "Beanie Babies: a case study in the engineering of a high involvement/relationship-prone brand," *The Journal of Product & Brand Management*, 9, no. 2 (2000): 78-98.

[23] Tomoko Takahashi and Brian Bremner, "Japan's Virtual Chick Spreads its Wings," *BusinessWeek*, March 10, 1997.

[24] "Solid Management Undefeated by Ebbing Boom: Having Learned a Lesson from Tamagotchi, Bandai Struggles to Surface Again," *Nikkei Business*, Feb. 2, 2003.

Chapter 8

Hello Kitty and the Ideology of Pleasure

Imagine, if you will, this admittedly surreal scenario: It is the year 2525, and, no, mankind is not alive. A catastrophic event has wiped us all out. What happened? Take your pick: Perhaps it was an asteroid and humankind couldn't find a Bruce Willis-like hero to save the day. Or maybe some particularly nasty and unforeseen biological attack by some terrorist group got really, really out of hand or we, as a species, just consumed our natural resources (and ourselves) into absolute oblivion. It doesn't much matter. Highly developed extraterrestrials from some outer constellation descend upon planet Earth. They are on a scouting mission, having concluded this third rock from the sun worthy of exploration. They quickly find evidence of advanced societies, though they also conclude that there was great inequality of wealth at the time of extinction, which they figured came early in the 21st century.

They discover all sorts of artifacts that suggest the most evolved species on Earth, at least in the wealthy and developed regions, had some very bizarre spending habits. Thanks to assorted time capsules the species had left behind and crude digitally recorded archives, they find a baffling array of consumer goods that didn't seem central to everyday existence. Among the most inexplicable were things like Ronald McDonald Christmas tree ornaments, Barbie dolls, nipple lightening crème, a bottle of tablets that promised to make one's excrement odor free and diapers for a less-developed species called canines in the local vernacular.[1] Then on an archipelago off the far reaches of the Eurasian landmass they find the most mind-boggling archeological find of all. In a vault in the ruins of a city called Tokyo, they discover Hello Kitty. They puzzle over a doll in the form of a feline, but not realistically rendered the best they could tell. The doll has tiny eyes and a large, marshmallow-shaped head. It has no mouth for some baffling reason.

The image seemed to be replicated on all manner of consumer goods, thousands of them such as pens, panties, watches, cups, plates, chopsticks, toasters and stickers. Intriguingly, their reconnaissance in other parts of Asia, Europe and North America found evidence that the cult of Hello Kitty had spread. It was a major find, but caused plenty of consternation. The scouting team then broke out into a fierce debate about whether intelligent life had, indeed, really existed on Earth at all. Perhaps they had been misled. Or maybe intelligence levels had for some reason plummeted before extinction. They wondered if some sort of mass delusion had set into the most developed parts of this species that goods like Hello Kitty and other highly dispersed products, as well as images in a grouping of artifacts produced by a company called Disney, were really all that essential.

Well, you get the idea. Forget the musings of our otherworldly explorers for the moment. The fact is, it is patently obvious that we'd all get on just fine without Hello Kitty and a million other products that we consume and dispose everyday. And yet, Sanrio has a brand that has survived nearly three decades on the premise that a cute and precious image can be slapped on just about every product under the sun and get consumed and consumed again by millions of people across a broad section of the rich world. And that raises a lot of interesting questions. We have already delved into how Hello Kitty the brand has unique features that shatter conventional notions about marketing being a simple calculus of price and value. This cat makes all sorts of emotional connections to a loyal band of consumers who seem to migrate from one licensed product to another, whatever Sanrio can cook up next. And whether by design or accident she has many of the chief attributes that anthropologists think are essential to consumer behavior. And when it comes to marketing directly to the cognitive psychology of kids, Sanrio ranks among the best of them.

But brands need care and feeding, and sometimes a strategic rethink to meet the changing needs of consumers in, say, 2005, let alone 2525. Even global fashion icons like Hello Kitty run the risk of imploding without careful attention. Aside from considering whether this particular brand will survive or not, another puzzle to sort through is whether something *like* Hello Kitty — in short an image quintessentially cute and precious — will continue to have such a broad appeal in the global marketplace. In the case of this simplistic, moon-faced image, design trumps function. We obviously don't buy our children a plastic Hello Kitty-festooned toy microwave oven because we need one. And even if we did need one for whatever inane reason, we could fetch one far cheaper off the rack at Toys 'R' Us sans the mouthless feline. But we buy it from Sanrio or one of its licensees because our kids are screaming, "Mommy, pleeease!" And in her minimalist design lies something of a paradox: her simplicity manages to trigger a complex set of emotions both within individuals and across different market economies. There is a massive field of desire that surrounds this brand that offers up many insights for product designers and marketers alike. Noted one keen observer:

> She teaches the need to focus not just on different tastes within a certain "society" (however this term may be defined), but also on diverse attitudes within the same individual. Such inter-subjectivity is expressed, at least in the case of Hello Kitty, in two ways. The first is visible across generations. Through its marketing of Hello Kitty, Sanrio has made a concentrated effort to tie together within a single individual, different modes of self-presentation that chronologically correspond to girlhood, female adolescence, and womanhood: "cute", "cool", and "camp." That is, as an individual matures, appeals to nostalgia, encourages a reconnection with the past by buying certain products united by one leitmotif; same commodity, same individual, different ages/tastes/styles/desires. Obviously, such a strategy may reap enormous profits.[2]

MARX MEETS HELLO KITTY

If our otherworldly friends looked back at the history of human consumption, they might end up concluding that, in the rich world at least, people increasingly bought stuff not for survival, but on whimsy and the pursuit of pleasure. And that consumption habits changed as societies changed. Lavish consumption isn't an option, of course, for the poorest fifth of humanity, which consume only 1.3% of private expenditures. (In contrast, the top fifth, the high-income economies of North America, Europe and Asia account for 86%.[3]) Suffice it to say, desperately poor countries such as Afghanistan and Somalia aren't major markets for Sanrio. But in rich economies, the purchase of non-essential and disposable items comes as naturally as breathing. Some might say that full-blown commercialized consumption is absolutely essential to continued growth in developed economies.

To Marxist-leaning critics, Hello Kitty and all other sorts of idle purchases are now part of the DNA of advanced market capitalism, a natural response to the crisis of overproduction.[4] In other words, the U.S., Western Europe and Japan produce so much surplus goods that companies and their marketing departments need to cook up all sorts of devilish manipulation gambits to convince us to buy. We are bombarded from every direction with subtle and not-so-subtle persuasion campaigns telling us how to spend our leisure time and stirring up desires to acquire the latest gadget, the latest accessory, the latest Hello Kitty what-ever. Said one advertising wag: "Advertising is the art of arresting the human intelligence just long enough to get money from it."[5]

In 2001, the British Broadcasting Corporation aired a documentary dubbed *Shopology*. The BBC interviewed psychologists around the world to gain insights into why individuals in the U.S., Europe and Japan consume as they do. There were some striking similarities regardless of the obvious culture differences. In a nutshell, brands help us define who we are, give us some sort of social definition and in some ways we consume to fashion some sort of idealized lifestyle we'd like to have. Of course, Marxist-leaning academics see this as the net result of a vast array of forces and ideas that drive the most sophisticated market economies on the planet. Or in the words of one such critic:

> The consumer revolution of the late 19th and early 20th centuries was caused in large part by a crisis in production; new technologies had resulted in production of more goods, but there were not enough people to buy them. Since production is such an essential part of the culture of capitalism, society quickly adapted to the crisis by convincing people to buy things, by altering basic institutions and even generating a new ideology of pleasure. The economic crisis of the late 19th century was solved, but at considerable expense to the

environment in additional waste that was created and resources that were consumed.[6]

Of course, a Marxist wouldn't be a Marxist if his line of analysis didn't conclude that there were self-destructive mechanisms and inherent contradictions built into the whole capitalist setup. The original pitch from Karl Marx and his sidekick Friedrich Engels, by the way, was that class struggle against the vise-like grip of the bourgeois crowd over capital and exploitation of the working class would inevitably and inexorably replace capitalism with a socialist society followed by the blissful state of Communism. Obviously, things didn't work out that way — or at least not yet. Now, quasi-Marxist types contend the working class has been lulled into mindless consumers at the hands of clever capitalists. But the bad guys will get it in the end because of the environmental wreckage that runaway consumerism does to the planet. What's more, rich-world lifestyles in New York, London, Paris and Tokyo come at the expense of a Third World that drifts into resentment and anger. We will leave that argument for another day. But the critics of market capitalism are right about one thing, whether it is particularly pernicious or not.

Hello Kitty is one of more ridiculous examples around of the need to fill up our leisure time in pleasurable ways, no matter how small and trivial. And from the larger viewpoint of companies like Sanrio, or even market-driven economies as a whole, convincing rational people to buy, consume and then buy a variation or upgrade of essentially the same product is an absolute necessity. Hello Kitty fills this void for a big cross-section of mostly female consumers in the rich world. Putting aside the luxury Kitty goods such as branded wristwatches and jewelry, the lion's share of Sanrio line are cheap trinkets that are cherished by kids but then are dispatched to the bottom of the toy chest or more likely end up in a landfill. Kitty litter, as it were.

Not surprisingly, some child development experts look aghast on how runaway consumerism is purportedly warping the values of children. One pediatrician writing in the *Singapore Medical Association Journal* in 2000 described an event detailed elsewhere in the book this way:

> I have seen people queuing up behind a sign placed by the fast-food chain that the Hello Kitty dolls are sold at this point. My colleagues have noticed that several of their office staff have arrived late to work because they had queued up for a doll. Many rubbish bins outside the fast-food chain were full of discarded food uneaten, because once the person queuing obtained the doll, the food became redundant. Some parents feel that they are displaying love to the children when they shower them with presents. They indulge their children's every craving. This is exacerbated by the highly successful advertising on television. The child becomes obsessed with the desire to own the object advertised. Their peers exert further pressure. Parents think they are doing their child a great favor by giving in to their demands.[7]

Elsewhere in this book, we have noted other Hello Kitty critics spanning from conservative social critics in Japan to Asian-American performance artists. We need to add one more category: Critics of unbridled consumerism, who fear the "want a lot — waste a lot" advanced market economies are destroying the planet and our values in the quest for style, instant gratification and the mindless pursuit of novelty. American consumers, of course, are at the forefront of this trend. According to one source on U.S. spending habits: "Since 1950, Americans, alone, have used more resources than everyone who ever lived before them. Each American individual uses up 20 tons of basic raw materials annually. Americans throw away seven million cars a year, two million plastic bottles an hour and enough aluminum cans annually to make six thousand DC-10 airplanes."[8]

And plenty of critics think the trend is accelerating as more and more companies design disposable goods, or goods that serve no essential purpose other than convenience, novelty and pleasure:

> Much of what gets thrown away is packaging, the provocatively designed wrappings that we have come to expect on nearly everything we purchase. But it is not all packaging. Increasingly, products that in the past would have been considered durables quickly find their way into the trash bin. These include wristwatches, telephones and other electronic devices, razors, pens, medical and hospital supplies, cigarette lighters, and recently, cameras. General Electric and GTE sell $25 lamps designed to be discarded when the bulbs burn out. Black and Decker sells a throwaway travel iron. From a marketing point of view, disposability is the golden goose. It conflates the act of using with that of using up, and promotes markets that are continually hungry for more.[9]

It is perhaps a little unfair to indict Sanrio for crimes against humanity because it created a simple, yet powerful, fashion design that seems to bring all sorts of people a bit of pleasure, camp novelty or comfort. Sanrio, after all, is out to make money, lots of it. And it has every right to do so. But then again, Hello Kitty symbolizes a weird kind of unbridled materialism. The world doesn't particularly need 20,000-plus Hello Kitty products. But rich economies need consumers willing to cast caution to the wind to pay extra for a Helly Kitty toaster, or a t-shirt with a corporate logo on it, or a sports utility vehicle loaded with extras to the max because that jerk down the street got one. Big economies like the U.S. and Japan rely on consumer spending for something like over 60% of their economic output. That means collectively the corporations and their legion of marketing researchers and advertising agencies need to keep producing and, more importantly, designing products to keep everybody with a credit card locked in the dogged pursuit of the next big thing.

There is no grand conspiracy here. Every company that sells a product or service is, after all, motivated by profit. But taken altogether, it adds up to this: Big economies are kind of addicted to steady and robust expansions of consumer spending and desire to secure their economic prosperity going forward. In that sense, the world does need Hello Kitty and all other powerful design images that compel people to spend, spend and spend some more.

IT'S THE DESIGN, STUPID!

But maybe design isn't as sinister as all that. Maybe it is the consumers who demand and crave beauty. The author and *New York Times* business columnist Virginia Postrel noted that, "given a modicum of stability and sustenance, human beings demand and create beauty in ritual, personal adornment in everyday objects. Five thousand years ago, Stone Age weavers living in Swiss swamps were working intricate, multicolored patterns into their textiles and using fruit pits to create beaded cloth. There was nothing utilitarian about this work, nothing that suggests a society focused on only lower order needs."[10] Hello Kitty's global success is a touchstone example of the increasingly crucial role that design, as opposed to what the product actually does or what functional need it satisfies, plays in economic competition between companies and product marketing. After all, Hello Kitty meets the classic definition of the renowned 1930s-era industrial designer Harold Van Doren: "Design is fundamentally the art of using lines, forms, tones, colors and textures to arouse an emotional reaction in the beholder."[11]

During the 1970s and 1980s, function was the prince of the realm. Companies spent a lot of time trying to differentiate their products by superior performances, a unique technology edge or functionality. Once the product was designed to specs and at an affordable price, the designers were brought in to make a refinement here, and a refinement there, but these were stylistic decisions and rather minor ones. Today, it is safe to say, design is the ultimate differentiator in many global product categories where there aren't huge gaps in quality. In automobiles, sure, Toyota and Honda cars probably still have an edge when it comes to manufacturing versus Ford or General Motors, but a lot more time is now spent in search of a sensational design and feel to separate their nameplates from the global pack. In information technology and consumer electronics, an MP3 player made by a small start-up in Seoul isn't all that different than one made by a colossus like Sony in its basic makeup. The same holds true for all sorts of computer printers, personal computers and mobile phones. Thus, a lot of companies big and small spend a lot of time conjuring up a killer design to build a wow factor among consumers.

Among global business people, Corporate Japan has always been respected for its overall excellence in manufacturing. That's still true today, despite a decade plus of economic stagnation at home. Less well known, perhaps, is the prowess of Japanese product design. Leave Hello Kitty aside and consider Sony. The company's product designers produced a smash hit in the computing world with a silver and lavender notebook computer. It boasted a unique magnesium alloy case and, with the possible exception of Apple's iMac, created quite a stir among consumers in Japan and North America in the late 1990s. None of this should come as too much of a surprise to those familiar with the aesthetic pleasure Japanese consumers take from the exterior or wrapping of all sorts of products and goods. Swing through the food bazaar of any Japanese department store and you will quickly grasp this point.

All sorts of foodstuffs — from cookies to rice crackers to tiny cakes — are often individually wrapped in shiny, decorated plastic packets and then sorted in another decorative and colored cardboard box with individual compartments.

Smoked and cooked meats with assorted cheeses or a bottle of wine, popular for gift-giving occasions, are encased in expensive looking and thick plastic vacuum packs and then placed on a bed of cloth or bubble wrap inside a thick and compartmentalized box or perhaps a small wicker gift basket. One writer, who wrote an entire book on the subject, has called Japan a "Wrapping Culture."[12] In other words, the exterior of a product — its presentation and design — matters greatly to Japanese sensibilities. A Western perception of the practice prepares us to regard wrapping as a means to obscure the object inside, whereas in a Japanese view, the function of wrapping is to refine the object, to add to it layers of meaning which could not be carried in its unwrapped form.[13]

The Japanese figured out long ago that aesthetics really add value to a product and some consumers are willing to pay a premium to get their hands on it. A toothbrush is a fairly mundane item. But a pink one with Hello Kitty on its handle makes it more desirable in the eyes of a child. Obviously, Sanrio is lucky to have the copyright to a global fashion icon. Yet it is also a brilliant example of how design really matters, be it a toaster or a digital videodisc player. Nor is cuteness the only way to go on this score. Some design critics make clear what consumers sense as aesthetic value in a product design can vary greatly:

> Aesthetics obviously involves beauty, but what we mean by beauty is itself fraught with ambiguity. People perceive some things as beautiful without regard to culture or context — asymmetrical faces, smooth surfaces, and specific color combinations. Along with this biologically based perception, there is a more contextual aesthetic sense. Something that looks novel may be interesting, or something familiar comforting, without regard to its beauty in some ideal sense … Some designs attract through emotional associations, whether personal or cultural. We enjoy some aesthetic elements more over time, as we develop a taste for them or explore more of

their pattern and depth. Some styles draw power from allusion or wit. Aesthetics is not an absolute. It is a discovery process — a search through trial and error, experimentation and response, for sensory elements that move or delight. That process is open-ended and competitive, and one in which standards are subjective.[14]

Hello Kitty seems to have a multifaceted impact on consumers, firing off different streams of meaning that for some are personal and cultural — and for others kind of cynical and subversive. As we explored earlier, the Internet is full of websites that exploit Sanrio's prized feline to promote pornography, back political causes or score rhetorical points for feminist causes or even religious ones. Among her fan base, there are all sorts of interesting crosscurrents, too. To girls and young teens, Hello Kitty is precious and comforting. To 30-something mothers in the U.S. and Japan, the image elicits feelings of nostalgia, a harkening back to some sort of lost innocence. Still others just think Hello Kitty is cool and want to be in on the joke.

MUSEUM OF BAD FADS

Despite Hello Kitty's phenomenal success so far, however, one must still ask whether this cat has the kind of legs to really go the distance and be relevant another three decades down the road. Undoubtedly, the most obvious example of a simple and sentimental design that sparked a global craze and then ended in history's junkyard of failed brands is the story of Smiley Face. Just how a yellow face with a broad black-lined smile and two tiny, rounded black eyes exploded on the scene in the late 1960s, is a fascinating tale. Its creator was Harvey. R. Ball, an independent commercial graphics arts designer and World War II veteran, who had served in Okinawa. Based in Worcester, Massachusetts, he designed the fabled Smiley

Face logo in 1963 for a local and newly merged insurance company that was in the grip of severe morale problems. The insurer asked Ball to design an in-house corporate logo to go along with a "friendship" campaign at the company. The symbol would go on buttons, desk cards and posters to liven up the place and encourage a little *esprit de corps* among the salesmen and executives at the State Mutual Life Assurance Company, as it was called back then. According to a website devoted to the memory of Ball, who passed away in 2001, and what's left of the Smiley movement:

> Ball drew a smile but, not satisfied with the result, he added two eyes — the left slightly larger than the right — and making a smiley face. The whole drawing he recalled later, took 10 minutes. He was paid $240 for the entire campaign, and never received any further profit from his smiley-face design. The smiley face attained a life of its own well beyond the company's walls. Harvey Ball's design sparked a fad that swept a nation in the early 1970s. By 1971, smiley face was the hottest selling image in the country: an estimated 50 million smiley buttons alone had been sold, and the image appeared on countless other products as well. Eventually, Smiley's popularity began to wane, and by the mid-1970s the fad was over.[15]

Ball never bothered to copyright the image, which depending on your point of view was either the commercial blunder of the century or an admirable bit of artistic integrity. Anyway, unprotected, the image steadily crept into the national marketplace and by the late 1960s manufacturers were slapping the image on earrings, lights and even Cartier goods. But somewhere along the way, the image lost its staying power. Some said the decision by some companies to add the slogan — Have a Nice Day! — to the image did it in. Overexposure certainly played a role, too. Finally, as a free-floating image not under any corporate control, there was no orchestrated marketing campaign to keep the design fresh, keep it relevant to changing consumer tastes and control the pace of its distribution. Could a similar fate be awaiting Hello Kitty, whose central message is basically let's bake cookies and be friends?

THE WAY OF SNOOPY

There is no denying that Sanrio founder Tsuji is considered something of a marketing legend around Tokyo. One rival even calls him "The God of *Kawaii*." In fact, he is probably the closest thing to a figure like Walt Disney in Japan. And he is greatly admired for assembling a massive marketing and licensing machine to back up the Hello Kitty franchise. But talk to some of his rivals around town and they openly wonder if Hello Kitty's glory days are over unless there is a pretty dramatic rethink of the brand. Another pressing issue is what will happen after Tsuji retires. Though robust and in good health, Tsuji is already 75 and can't play maestro at Sanrio many more years. It is no secret that his son, Kunihiko, has been tapped to take the company to the next level. In late 2002, the more cosmopolitan son, who has plenty of international experience and speaks fluent English, was promoted to executive vice president. It won't be an easy transition. Tsuji senior enjoys a cult following inside Sanrio and decision-making is heavily centralized, which is a polite way of saying it is the founder's way or the highway. Kunihiko, other marketing executives in Tokyo insist, needs to push the company toward a more systematic way of managing and evaluating the Hello Kitty brand.

One such figure willing to talk openly about the challenges Sanrio faces is Hidetoshi Iwabuchi, managing director of United Media K.K., which promotes and licenses the Peanuts' cast of characters in Japan. Over the years, Iwabuchi has worked for consumer-product giants such as Procter & Gamble

Co. and Kao Corp. of Japan. He has lived in Los Angeles and New York and, as a younger man, he studied Peanuts comic strips to improve his vocabulary, knowledge of idiomatic phrasing and the Charles Schulz brand of irony and family values.

Whereas Sanrio has intentionally kept Hello Kitty's character development at a minimum, United Media has worked hard to flesh out the Peanuts characters, particularly Snoopy, for Japanese consumers. In terms of turnover and popularity, Snoopy typically lags behind Hello Kitty, though not by much. And Iwabuchi and his team have consciously tried to associate the Peanuts gang with positive educational and family values. United Media worked with noted Japanese pianist Takashi Obara to produce a compact disc called *Piano de Snoopy* with compositions inspired by the characters. And there have been books published that feature Peanuts comic strips in English with Japanese translations and commentaries about the deeper meanings of the characters. Make no mistake: United Media has a pretty extensive licensing network designed to move merchandise and make truckloads of yen, though nothing on the scale of Sanrio. You can see Snoopy product tie-ins with Baskin-Robbins, the ice cream retail chain. One can buy a Snoopy doll in samurai garb or a Mitsubishi Pajero Mini Snoopy edition with the "Flying Ace" on the spare-tire cover mounted on the back of this sports utility vehicle.

Yet the core strategy is to link Snoopy with non-materialistic values for the most part. Said Iwabuchi: "Snoopy and Hello Kitty offer up different kinds of lifestyles: Hello Kitty fans carry Louis Vuitton handbags and Burberry scarves, while Snoopy fans in Japan wear second-hand clothes."[16] The advantage, he said, is that Snoopy has a much larger market of consumers rather than the well-heeled types that lavish Hello Kitty artifacts on their kids. Unlike Sanrio, United Media keeps a tight rein on its distribution outlets and is careful not to let the Peanuts gang get too much commercial exposure. "We aren't trying to be the biggest character goods player in

Japan right away. We want to increase our business gradually." Echoing comments Tsuji has also made, he said, "A brand is kind of like a balloon, you don't want to blow it up too fast." Though Iwabuchi greatly admires Tsuji, he said it is time for Sanrio to take a more methodological approach to marketing instead of the straight-from-the-gut approach of the past. "They need to be thinking of what they should be doing 10 years from now," he said. Iwabuchi also noted that careful market research of what consumers admire about Hello Kitty would basically yield this: Not much, save that she is really, really cute and precious. As a result, Sanrio must somehow figure out a way to define this cat with more positive associations among the buying public, he suggested. Perhaps Sanrio should capitalize on its popularity with celebrities and develop a marketing campaign using female stars in their 20s and 30s, notables who young women might find praiseworthy for their achievements in the arts or popular culture.

HELLO KITTY AND COMMERCIAL CIVILIZATION

Whether Hello Kitty lives on will, of course, depend on a myriad of factors: Tactical marketing decisions by Sanrio, changing consumer values within rich country markets and so on. Just as modern marketers can't predict the tipping point of a fad with exact precision, so too, it is difficult to say with any certainty whether a brand will be around 10 or 20 years from now, despite the best efforts of a company to keep the magic going. Far more certain, though, is the probability that cuteness will live on as an important aesthetic value and continue to be of keen interest to the marketing pros in Japan, the U.S. and Europe. To be sure, it will be one of many possible emotional connections among consumers that marketing teams will try to tether to their products. Sex likely will always sell, as will irony and other marketing/emotive strategies not yet dreamed of.

Yet cute power, be it employed to sell the latest Beanie Baby or introduce feel-good emotional design properties to a blender, probably will continue to creep into the modern marketing landscape. The truth is, most of us, to some degree, need cute-looking stuff, a Smiley-Face radiance in design, to make up for the more garish, commercialized and, frankly, alienating aspects of living in a high-consumption society. This isn't an argument against prosperity, which is by and large a good thing. But the flipside is the somewhat obvious truth that even in rich and stable societies, where individuals are bombarded daily by commercially inspired images of what the true idealized lifestyle should be, existence can be a little disorientating. During the last decade of the 20th century, out of the echo chamber between mass media and pop sociology and psychology, emerged the concept of Affluenza, a play on the words affluence and influenza. It is basically an epidemic of over-consumption, in which individuals feel a heat blast of desire to consume from a deluge of marketing persuasion campaigns and the ultimate chump's game of keeping up with the Joneses and the Watanabes.

In its mildest forms, maybe it is a foolish impulse to buy a $68,000 Porsche Cayenne S sports utility vehicle that likely will never make it out of suburban New York or the posh, outlying communities of Western Tokyo. Or perhaps in some misguided notion of what parental love is all about, we cave into just about every consumer desire of our kids. They end up with a room full of Hello Kitty regalia or enough Hot Wheels tracks to span the Rainbow Bridge over Tokyo Bay. Then again, maybe these kids have just had their tickets punched for a lifetime pass on the consumption express. In more virulent forms, once rational consumers get on the cosmic hamster wheel, they take on massive debts to buy stuff they can't afford and then work themselves into a state of stupor and are thus unable to enjoy the object of their desire.

Rich economies fixated on high-speed consumption turn lifecycle rituals such as birthdays, the passing of the seasons, and all manner of religious and secular holidays into gift-giving occasions — or, more accurately, societal obligations to consume.

And then there is the disconnect between the idealized lifestyles we mentally aspire to and the reality back in the here and now. Consider modern Japan, which to the uninitiated in the West is probably still thought of as the land of tea ceremonies, highly ritualized arts like *kabuki* and flower arrangements. You can, of course, find that kind of high culture. But everyday life is far different. For the salaryman and office lady commuting every day, the visual landscape is overwhelmed by subway banners peddling cuties spilling out of their bikinis to draw attention to soft-porn *manga*, perfectly accessorized models on the cover of smart fashion magazines, young foreign surfer studs peddling cigarettes and robust middle-aged celebrities downing mugs of Kirin Lager and Asahi Dry. The urban nightscape of Shibuya and Shinjuku is lit up by enormous neon and digital displays showering even more messages designed to entice and consume. Japanese newspapers and magazines are brimming with stories about teenage girls in dating clubs that link them with middle-aged men to engage in *enjo kosai*, compensated sex. They do so to earn yen to buy a luxury handbag and other forms of frivolous consumption.

One might mention as well how the Upper East and West sides of New York are increasingly turning into mini-malls as national chains such as Blockbusters' video and Border's books push out independent retailers that, by their presence, often gave certain streets a unique feel. Or one could rant endlessly about the soullessness of suburban America, where mega-malls and jammed traffic grids force folks to spend more leisure time in their cars en route to the next shopping excursion. According to one writer on that topic, "In 1986, America still had more high schools than shopping centers.

Less than 15 years later, we have more than twice as many shopping centers as high schools. In the Age of Affluenza … shopping centers have supplanted churches as a symbol of cultural values. In fact, 70% of us visit malls each week, more than those who attend houses of worship. Our equivalent of Gothic cathedrals is the mega-malls."[17]

The point here is not to rail against consumerism. Plenty of folks across the world heed Aristotle's advice about, "moderation in all things." Parents can buy their kids a Hello Kitty doll, suntanned in a grass hoola-hoop skirt, and still raise well-adjusted kids. In fact, the cute style perfected by Sanrio does have some appeal to marketers. Design that makes us feel good in some way, establishes some emotional connection with the goods we buy, is something marketing types increasingly think about.

Of course Japan did not invent cuteness, nor does it own a monopoly on the sweet and the precious. But they have come closest to perfecting it as a marketing tool or strategy to engender powerful emotions of longing, comfort, sentimentality and nostalgia, often motivating consumers to buy stuff. Hello Kitty is a global phenomenon and for all the anti-cute emotions she stokes among her critics, she is one of the more thought-provoking brands around.

You can sneer at the global fad surrounding this cat; you can rage against it, too. Yet for those with any intellectual curiosity about marketing theory, Japanese pop culture and why humankind desires such things — why we consume as we do — you can't really ignore her. For this simple, feline form with a red ribbon, button nose and no mouth has managed to connect with millions of consumers around the planet. She has deep reservoirs of meaning. She is consumerism incarnate. And, for the moment at least, resistance is futile. So, we end our odyssey into all things Hello Kitty by wishing this cat all the best. May she finish out her years as a brand eating yummy cookies with her sister Mimmy and sharing good times with her very, very best friends: Tim and Tammy, Mory and Rory,

Tippy and Tiny Chum and the whole gang of Sanrio-inspired critters.

ENDNOTES

[1] Yes, this stuff really does exist. See "The Museum of Weird Consumer Culture" at: http://www.indiana.edu/~wanthro/museum.htm.

[2] McVeigh, 225-245.

[3] United Nations Development Program, Human Development Report, 1998.

[4] A good summary full of links to other sources on this school of market capitalist critics can be found at: http://www.globalissues.org/TradeRelated/Consumption.asp.

[5] Ben H. Bagdikan, *The Media Monopoly* (Boston: Beacon Press, 2000), 185.

[6] Richard Robbins, *Global Problems and the Culture of Capitalism,* (London: Pearson, Allyn and Bacon, 1999), 210.

[7] Dr. Kenneth Lyen, Hello Kitty, *Singapore Medical Association Journal*, Volume 32, Issue 2, Feb. 2000.

[8] For more statistics on Affluenza go to *http://www.pbs.org/kcts/affluenza/diag/diag.html.*

[9] Stuart Ewen, "Waste a Lot, Want a Lot: Our All-Consuming Quest for Style" at http://www.geocities.com/su_englit/ewen_waste.html.

[10] Virginia Postrel, "The Aesthetic Economy: Beauty is Not Skin Deep," The Milken Institute, Fourth Quarter, 1999: 14.

[11] Ibid., 12.

[12] Joy Hendry, *Wrapping Culture: Politeness, Presentation and Power in Japan and other Societies* (Oxford: Oxford University Press, 1993).

[13] Ibid.

[14] Postrel, 14.

[15] To learn more about Harvey Ball go to: http://www.worldsmileday.com/about_smiley.htm.

[16] Iwabuchi, personal interview, Oct. 2002.

[17] Wann, de Graaf Naylor, *Affluenza: The All-Consuming Epidemic* (San Francisco: Berrett-Koehler, 2001).

Index